EMPOWERED

(in)courage Book List

DEVOTIONALS

*Take Heart: 100 Devotions to Seeing
God When Life's Not Okay*

Empowered: More of Him for All of You

TRADE BOOKS

The Simple Difference by Becky Keife

BIBLE STUDIES

*Courageous Simplicity:
Living in the Simple Abundance of Jesus*

*Courageous Joy:
Delight in God through Every Season*

*Courageous Influence:
Embrace the Way God Made You for Impact*

*Courageous Kindness:
Live the Simple Difference Right Where You Are*

Create in Me a Heart of Hope (available March 2022)

Create in Me a Heart of Peace (available August 2022)

Create in Me a Heart of Wisdom (available January 2023)

Create in Me a Heart of Mercy (available May 2023)

For more resources, visit incourage.me.

EMPOWERED

More of Him for All of You

**Mary Carver, Grace P. Cho,
and Anna E. Rendell**

Revell
a division of Baker Publishing Group
www.RevellBooks.com

Published by Revell
a division of Baker Publishing Group
PO Box 6287, Grand Rapids, MI 49516-6287
www.revellbooks.com

Printed in the United States of America

Library of Congress Cataloging-in-Publication Data
Names: Carver, Mary (Writer), author. | Cho, Grace P., author. | Rendell, Anna E., author.
Title: Empowered : more of Him for all of you / Mary Carver, Grace P. Cho and Anna E. Rendell.
Description: Grand Rapids : Revell, a division of Baker Publishing Group, [2022] | Includes index.
Identifiers: LCCN 2021020300 | ISBN 9780800738167 | ISBN 9781493434312 (ebook)
Subjects: LCSH: Power (Christian theology)—Biblical teaching. | Power (Christian theology)—Meditations. | Self-actualization (Psychology)— Religious aspects—Christianity—Miscellanea.
Classification: LCC BS680.P5 C37 2022 | DDC 242/.2—dc23
LC record available at https://lccn.loc.gov/2021020300

(in)courage is represented by Alive Literary Agency, www.aliveliterary.com.

Baker Publishing Group publications use paper produced from sustainable forestry practices and post-consumer waste whenever possible.

22   23   24   25   26   27   28   7   6   5   4   3   2   1

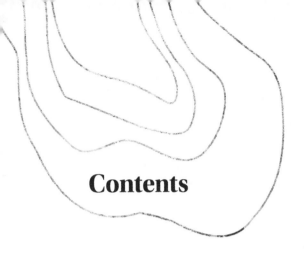

Contents

Contents

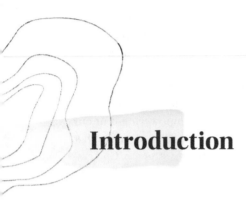

Introduction

The word *empowerment* brings to mind motivational speakers and the self-help section of a bookstore. Messages from the stage and page tend to run along the lines of "If you believe in yourself, you can do anything!" It's an inspiring slogan in the moment, but its energy fizzles out in the long run. It falls short of what we truly long for—to be empowered in the fullness of who we are.

The problem is that we've learned to compartmentalize ourselves—our physical bodies, our mental health, our emotional well-being, our relationships with one another, and our faith in God. We seek empowerment in each category by watching fitness gurus on YouTube or listening to Enneagram podcasts, reading books by celebrity pastors or trying the latest health food.

But what often happens is that we prioritize certain parts of our being over others because it feels more spiritual or urgent. We might nourish our souls but neglect to eat well and drink plenty of water. We might exercise our minds but lack meaningful friendships. When we do this, we become lopsided in our being, forgetting that every aspect of our lives is important to cultivate because God is in it all.

God cares about our whole being because He, who is spirit, became flesh in order to dwell among us (John 1:14). Jesus, who is fully God, took on Himself the vulnerability and beauty of being human. He enjoyed eating meals and napped when He was tired. He wept when His friend died and raged in anger at injustice. And His work of redemption includes the restoration of our bodies, minds, and souls.

God is invested in our wholeness and the empowerment of our whole being. This involves more than "You go, girl!" statements that lead us to believe we can do everything in our own strength. God empowers us to be all that He's made us to be by the truth of His Word and the indwelling of the Holy Spirit.

This book is designed to incorporate the five major components of our being—physical, mental, emotional, relational, and spiritual. The sixty Scripture passages and devotions invite you to see from different angles how God empowers us, and each day ends with prayer and reflection questions to deepen the learning. Each Scripture and devotion will be labeled according to which of the five major components it generally falls under.

As you read this book, may you be empowered in every part of your being to live fully as God created you to be.

Emotional

Empowered to Be Seen

> The angel of the LORD found Hagar near a spring in the desert; it was the spring that is beside the road to Shur. And he said, "Hagar, slave of Sarai, where have you come from, and where are you going?"
>
> "I'm running away from my mistress Sarai," she answered.
>
> Then the angel of the LORD told her, "Go back to your mistress and submit to her." The angel added, "I will increase your descendants so much that they will be too numerous to count." . . .
>
> She gave this name to the LORD who spoke to her: "You are the God who sees me," for she said, "I have now seen the One who sees me."
>
> Genesis 16:7–10, 13

I recognize myself in her. She is busy, dodging people left and right as she sets the table. She's been up on her feet all day preparing the meal—the feast, really—for the family gathering, but she's only halfway done. She moves deftly between people, as if she's dancing, stirring the pot while smiling and chatting effortlessly with the aunts and uncles, grabbing garnishes from the fridge and large glass platters from the pantry.

I offer my help, but she waves me off to go hang out with the young people. She's got it covered, and she just wants me to relax and have fun; I only want the same for her.

When everyone else has served themselves and is happily gorging on her delicious food, she goes around and makes sure they all have what they need: something to drink, napkins, second helpings. I catch her looking around, surveying the crowd, and finally satisfied, she gets a plate for herself and pulls up a chair at the edge of the table. She settles in, wincing from the pain in her knees. Her apron is still on, her duties not quite finished.

She sends each family home with enough leftovers for another meal the next day. Even though I don't witness the rest of her night, I know she'll spend the next hour or so cleaning the mess we left, wiping down counters, vacuuming crumbs left by little ones, and getting her house back to normal.

She's the invisible force that carries everyone else. It's what she'll do at every gathering because it's expected of her culturally, societally. She knows no other way, and though I'm of a different generation, I feel the same pressures. I've learned to be invisible, to serve and help until I wince in pain at the end.

It's the quiet suffering that's considered part of the job of being a woman. Though it isn't so in every culture or in every family, the idea that women can and should carry more is almost universally accepted as true. We are the ones who sacrifice our careers, our time, our space, and our bodies on the altar of our families, of marriage and motherhood. It's complicated and nuanced, but for many women, including myself, the expectation to bear it all quietly is how we often become invisible. We lose ourselves in the needs of others and are left feeling lonely, rejected, and perhaps even discarded.

Hagar understood. She had been used by her masters, Abraham and Sarah, to bear them a child. But when the pregnancy created enmity between the two women, Sarah treated Hagar so harshly that Hagar ran away to the wilderness, unable to take any more.

And this was where God met her, where He saw her—abused, alone, vulnerable. But even before that moment, He had already heard her cries and knew her pain.

And He sees us too. When we're overlooked, when others take advantage of us, when we pour out until we're empty, God meets us. He strengthens us to challenge oppressive expectations, and He sustains us to keep going even when circumstances cannot change.

Our God is El Roi, the One who sees us and does not pass us by. He notices every sacrifice and every ounce of love poured out. His eye on us tells us we are worthy of being seen.

EL ROI, *thank You for seeing me even when I've become nearly invisible to others. Though the expectations that culture and society place on me as a woman are unfair, You help me. You empower me to break free from what is not right. Thank You for noticing me today and calling me valuable. Amen.*

REFLECT

What are some circumstances in your life that make you feel unseen?

How does Hagar's story empower you to value yourself as God values you?

Empowered to Be Beautiful

He has made everything beautiful in its time.

Ecclesiastes 3:11

So God created human beings in his own image.
In the image of God he created them;
male and female he created them.

Genesis 1:27 NLT

I have two daughters, one with dark eyes and brown curls and one with blue eyes and straight blonde hair. Both are spunky, sweet, a little sassy, and beyond beautiful. Their eyes sparkle, their smiles are huge, and their hearts are genuine and dear.

When I look at them, I see beauty. Sometimes I wonder what it would take for me to look in the mirror and see myself the same way.

Losing the baby weight? Clearing up that annoying adult acne? A fashionable haircut? A cute new outfit? A full night's sleep to brighten up the dark under-eye circles? Whitened teeth and full makeup? Sure, these things could all help me feel pretty, but even then, I still feel like beauty is unattainable these days.

You see, right now I have a baby and three older kids to keep track of. I'm likely unshowered, wearing last night's pajamas, and covered in baby spit-up. I don't have time or motivation to put on makeup or blow-dry my hair, and my non-maternity clothes don't fit yet. I don't feel back to beautiful, that's for sure.

I think this is the part where I'm supposed to chirp, *But it doesn't matter, because my baby is worth every pound and every day of dark circles!* Of course he is. Without question. Duh. I also think I'm supposed to say very little about external beauty: *It's the heart that matters. Beauty is in the eye of the beholder. Charm is deceptive and beauty is fleeting and all that.*

However, I would argue that external beauty does matter and that there is indeed value in our feeling beautiful. After all, God created us in His own image, and Scripture says He makes all things beautiful. And since we are each created by God, those words apply to us—even on the days when it's hard to see our own beauty.

The beauty we see in nature stops us in our tracks and takes our breath away. The glory of a sunset. The reds and golds of changing autumn leaves. The joyous smiles on my children's sweet faces.

It is okay, friends, to look for and cultivate beauty and to feel beautiful.

One summer when I was working as a camp counselor, my roommate was applying a light amount of makeup, and I mentioned that I'd left my makeup at home. To be clear, I was incredibly proud of this fact—and not in a good way. I was proud in a haughty, my-priorities-are-clearer-than-yours way. She paused, then gently said, "It's okay to embrace your beauty and femininity." That was at least twenty years ago, and the moment is still with me.

When God said He made us beautiful, it's because we reflect Him. We are created in His image, so we are beautiful from the get-go. End of story. Nothing we can do will increase our inherent beauty. It's one of God's gifts to us, and we can embrace it.

So I say it's good to recognize the ways God has made each of us beautiful. Indeed, we *should* do this. Maybe it's the way your eyes disappear when you smile big or the tone of your skin. Maybe your lashes curl up on their own or you have perfectly aligned toes or long graceful fingers. Maybe it's your laugh, silvery and pealing, or your hair, whether wavy and short or straight and long. Whatever our physical traits, God imagined, formed, and created us beautifully. And He wants us to recognize that, because in seeing and accepting our own beauty, we see God's too.

LORD, *just as I see Your beauty reflected in the sunset, my kids, and other aspects of Your creation, may I see it also reflected in myself. I want to be able to look in the mirror and call every part of myself good as You do. Help me to recognize the beauty You have empowered me to live into. Amen.*

REFLECT

On days when it's a stretch to see, how can you focus on the beauty of God within your own self?

Is it easier for you to see the reflection of God within others? Why?

The Power of Beauty

Esther 2:2–11, 17–18; 5:1–5

Then the king's personal attendants proposed, "Let a search be made for beautiful young virgins for the king. Let the king appoint commissioners in every province of his realm to bring all these beautiful young women into the harem at the citadel of Susa. Let them be placed under the care of Hegai, the king's eunuch, who is in charge of the women; and let beauty treatments be given to them. Then let the young woman who pleases the king be queen instead of Vashti." This advice appealed to the king, and he followed it.

Now there was in the citadel of Susa a Jew of the tribe of Benjamin, named Mordecai son of Jair, the son of Shimei, the son of Kish, who had been carried into exile from Jerusalem by Nebuchadnezzar king of Babylon, among those taken captive with Jehoiachin king of Judah. Mordecai had a cousin named Hadassah, whom he had brought up because she had neither father nor mother. This young woman, who was also known as Esther, had a lovely figure and was beautiful. Mordecai had taken her as his own daughter when her father and mother died.

When the king's order and edict had been proclaimed, many young women were brought to the citadel of Susa and put under the care of Hegai. Esther also was taken to the king's palace and entrusted to Hegai, who had charge of the harem. She pleased him and won his favor. Immediately he provided her with her beauty treatments and special food. He assigned to her seven female attendants selected from the king's palace and moved her and her attendants into the best place in the harem.

Esther had not revealed her nationality and family background, because Mordecai had forbidden her to do so. Every day he walked back and forth near the courtyard of the harem to find out how Esther was and what was happening to her. . . .

Now the king was attracted to Esther more than to any of the other women, and she won his favor and approval more than any of the other virgins. So he set a royal crown on her head and made her queen instead of Vashti. And the king gave a great banquet, Esther's banquet, for all his nobles and officials. He proclaimed a holiday throughout the provinces and distributed gifts with royal liberality. . . .

On the third day Esther put on her royal robes and stood in the inner court of the palace, in front of the king's hall. The king was sitting on his royal throne in the hall, facing the entrance. When he saw Queen Esther standing in the court, he was pleased with her and held out to her the gold scepter that was in his hand. So Esther approached and touched the tip of the scepter.

Then the king asked, "What is it, Queen Esther? What is your request? Even up to half the kingdom, it will be given you."

"If it pleases the king," replied Esther, "let the king, together with Haman, come today to a banquet I have prepared for him."

"Bring Haman at once," the king said, "so that we may do what Esther asks."

So the king and Haman went to the banquet Esther had prepared.

GOD, *thank You that every part of my being is of value to You. You see worth in my beauty. Help me to believe it too. Amen.*

REFLECT

What can you learn about God's perspective of beauty from this Scripture passage?

What is God saying to you about being empowered to be beautiful?

Empowered to Be Hopeful

Rest in God alone, my soul,
for my hope comes from him.
He alone is my rock and my salvation,
my stronghold; I will not be shaken.

Psalm 62:5–6 CSB

Until recently, I had never struggled with hope. Though the years had taught me to be more of a realist than a pure optimist, and though I'd walked through many truly painful seasons and circumstances, my trust in God never wavered. And because I trusted God, I remained hopeful for the future.

But two years ago, my good friend's daughter was hurt. She was hurt in a way that no child should ever experience, no mother should ever imagine. She was hurt in a way that's not my story to tell. But what became part of my own story was the way my faith was shaken as I walked through this darkness with my friend.

To my friend, I stayed strong in faith that God was with her and her little girl, certain that justice would prevail, and hopeful that her daughter would survive without scars. In my heart, though, I became a crumbling, raging, hopeless mess. I sobbed and screamed, asking God how He could allow such a thing to happen, begging Him to explain where He was and why He didn't intervene. I trembled and whispered only to myself that maybe some things don't work out in the end, that maybe God isn't completely in control.

As much as that incident and my subsequent deep sadness messed with my heart and mind, what really threw me for a loop was the fear that my faith had been unfounded all these years. What shook me most was the fact that I was shaken. After all, while I might struggle with a whole lot of things, hope had never been one of them! Even when I had to work overtime to choose joy or be patient, I'd always had my general hopefulness to fall back on. Now, though, I wasn't sure how to hope.

I'd like to tell you that I dove into Scripture and prayer the moment I realized the depth of my doubt and despair, that I went straight to the Lord with my hurt and my missing hope. But I didn't. Instead, I sank deeper into confusion and chaos as everything I'd previously pinned my hope and trust on seemed to slip away each time I thought about my friend's grief. I turned my questioning eyes on myself, wondering how strong my faith had been in the first place if it could be so shaken by someone else's pain.

I finally broke down and told another friend about my struggle. Understanding how hopeless I was feeling, she placed her hands on my shoulders and prayed that God would protect and heal my friend and her daughter—and that He would comfort and heal me as well. I didn't have to tell her I was broken; she knew. And when I was unable to ask God for help, she asked for me.

My friend's simple prayer became my breakthrough. Her hope helped me find my own hope again. It gave me the gentle push I needed to ask God to remind me of the truths that never change—that He is good, that He loves us, that He is with us and will never leave us. I asked God to rebuild my foundation and to help me remember that my faith is *in Him*, not in my faith or myself. I asked God to show me how strong and steadfast He is so that I could in turn share that vision with anyone else who needed it.

And of course, God did. Little by little, the ground underneath me felt less shaky, and I could stand with confidence again, trusting the firm foundation only the Lord can give. The promises of other people, a false sense of safety or security based on humanity's goodness, and even my own faith are shifting sands that won't hold up to the storms of this world. But Jesus, our Rock and our unshakable foundation? He will always be there—through the storms and when the winds finally subside.

When you feel yourself begin to slip and slide, when you doubt and then wonder how you could possibly doubt, don't despair! God hasn't changed. He hasn't left you behind—and He won't. No matter how shaky you feel, God's still here and He's still holding steady. Ask Him to help you believe. Ask God to give you hope—in Him, in His promises and plans, in the story He is writing for you and for your loved ones. And even when the storm rages, God will give you hope to hold on to and to share.

GOD, *I feel shaky sometimes, unsure of myself and of my hope in You. Please forgive me when the doubts are louder than Your love for me and for those I love. Renew my faith, rebuild my foundation, and give me hope to hold on to and to share with others. Amen.*

REFLECT

What have you built your foundation on?

Where in your life do you need more hope?

Empowered to Cheer Each Other On

If one part suffers, all the parts suffer with it, and if one part is honored, all the parts are glad.

1 Corinthians 12:26 NLT

My phone dings, and I see her text: "Could you read something I wrote? I don't know if it's any good, but I wanted to see if you could just take a look and tell me what you think."

I could hear the hesitancy in her words and how much courage it took for her to ask. We had met each other at a conference, and from our brief interactions, I knew she had stories to tell, pain to express, and wisdom to lead with. We noticed each other in a breakout session for writers interested in getting published, and afterward we talked in hushed tones about our hopes for where our writing would go. The writing world and its nuances were new for us, and we parted ways holding those hopes for each other.

Eventually, I became an editor, and I watched from afar as her leadership took her places. I witnessed her voice become louder and stronger as she processed the current social climate through her newsletters. I could see that she was becoming freer, more herself, and less afraid of what people would think of her.

And so was I.

Her text was an unexpected but pleasant surprise. She shared how she had been keeping up with me as well and thought she'd take a step of faith by reaching out. I was honored to be entrusted with a first read of her writing, and I agreed to take a look and get back to her soon.

I wasn't prepared for her gift with words. She wrote with precision and power, beauty and hope. She didn't shy away from naming her pain, and her pastoral and prophetic leadership shined through her stories. I was blown away by her natural talent, and I texted her immediately to tell her so.

She responded, "Really? You think so?" Her lack of confidence boggled my mind, and I sent back ten yeses in all caps with way too many exclamation marks. I assured her I wasn't just saying it because she was a friend. I genuinely believed she should be writing and getting published.

We went back and forth about her essay a couple of times, but it wasn't until years later that I received another text: "The essay we worked on got published in a book!"

I squealed in delight at this news. Her success wasn't only about her but also about the many other women—particularly women of color—who would see her name in a book and know what was possible for them too. Her joy was my joy.

First Corinthians 12:26 says, "If one part suffers, all the parts suffer with it, and if one part is honored, all the parts are glad." And Romans 12:15 simply says, "Be happy with those who are happy" (NLT). In Christ, we are intricately intertwined and interdependent on one another. Because we are made for community and placed in community, we cannot separate our grief or our joy from that of others.

In a world and time when social media and celebrity culture hype certain people over others, it's easy to feel envious of someone else's success. Those feelings are understandable and shouldn't be shoved down in order to celebrate others. Instead, we can bring our honest selves before God, confessing our hurt, disappointment, and anger, acknowledging our own desire for success, and letting God be a balm for us. He can realign our hearts to His, remind us that together we make up the body of Christ, and teach us to be glad when another is honored.

We can be countercultural by cheering each other on, and in doing so we participate in the joy that God has for us all.

I relished in my friend's news. I was so proud of her work, her persistence, and her increasing belief in herself. I had the privilege of watching her growth like a time lapse of a seed becoming a plant, and my delight was just a glimpse of God's rejoicing over her. And from my vantage point, I could see that this was just the beginning.

GOD, *thank You that there isn't a limited amount of joy to go around and that one person's success doesn't cancel out another's. You are not a God of scarcity but of abundance. I confess that there are times when I have a hard time cheering someone else on when I'm not in the same place or position as they are. But I want to learn to participate in their joy as You are inviting me to do. Thank You for creating us to be the body of Christ so that gladness can be multiplied instead of hoarded. Amen.*

REFLECT

How has someone gone above and beyond in cheering for you?

How is God inviting you to cheer on someone in your life?

The Power of Celebrating in Community

Luke 1:26–56

In the sixth month of Elizabeth's pregnancy, God sent the angel Gabriel to Nazareth, a town in Galilee, to a virgin pledged to be married to a man named Joseph, a descendant of David. The virgin's name was Mary. The angel went to her and said, "Greetings, you who are highly favored! The Lord is with you."

Mary was greatly troubled at his words and wondered what kind of greeting this might be. But the angel said to her, "Do not be afraid, Mary; you have found favor with God. You will conceive and give birth to a son, and you are to call him Jesus. He will be great and will be called the Son of the Most High. The Lord God will give him the throne of his father David, and he will reign over Jacob's descendants forever; his kingdom will never end."

"How will this be," Mary asked the angel, "since I am a virgin?"

The angel answered, "The Holy Spirit will come on you, and the power of the Most High will overshadow you. So the holy one to be born will be called the Son of God. Even Elizabeth your relative is going to have a child in her old age, and she who was said to be unable to conceive is in her sixth month. For no word from God will ever fail."

"I am the Lord's servant," Mary answered. "May your word to me be fulfilled." Then the angel left her.

At that time Mary got ready and hurried to a town in the hill country of Judea, where she entered Zechariah's home and greeted Elizabeth. When Elizabeth heard Mary's greeting, the baby leaped in her womb, and Elizabeth was filled with the Holy Spirit. In a loud voice she exclaimed: "Blessed are you among women, and blessed is the child you will bear! But why am I so favored, that the mother of my Lord should come to me? As soon as the sound of your greeting reached my ears, the baby in my womb leaped for joy. Blessed is she who has believed that the Lord would fulfill his promises to her!"

And Mary said:

> "My soul glorifies the Lord
> and my spirit rejoices in God my Savior,
> for he has been mindful
>   of the humble state of his servant.
> From now on all generations will call me blessed,
> for the Mighty One has done great things for me—
>   holy is his name.
> His mercy extends to those who fear him,
>   from generation to generation.
> He has performed mighty deeds with his arm;
>   he has scattered those who are proud in their inmost
>   thoughts.
> He has brought down rulers from their thrones
>   but has lifted up the humble.
> He has filled the hungry with good things
>   but has sent the rich away empty.
> He has helped his servant Israel,
>   remembering to be merciful
> to Abraham and his descendants forever,
>   just as he promised our ancestors."

Mary stayed with Elizabeth for about three months and then returned home.

GOD, *thank You that I am not meant to walk alone in this life. Thank you for the community You've placed me in right now to journey alongside in times of both hardship and celebration. Amen.*

REFLECT

What can you learn about God's desire for us to be community from this Scripture passage?

What is God saying to you about the power of celebrating together?

Empowered to Be Known

O Lord, you have examined my heart
    and know everything about me.
You know when I sit down or stand up.
    You know my thoughts even when I'm far away.
You see me when I travel
    and when I rest at home.
    You know everything I do.
You know what I am going to say
    even before I say it, Lord. . . .
How precious are your thoughts about me, O God.
    They cannot be numbered!
I can't even count them;
    they outnumber the grains of sand!

Psalm 139:1–4, 17–18 NLT

My degree is in youth and family ministry, and my first job fresh out of college was working with middle and high school students as the director of youth ministries at a large church. As a former camp counselor, I tried to bring those faith experiences into practice in a congregational setting. For instance, we dug a firepit and had bonfires throughout the summer. And it was at one of these bonfires that I shared a favorite devotion I'd used throughout my camp counseling ministry.

I had each student lick their fingertip and swipe it through the dirt under their feet, then told them to count the grains of sand now stuck to their fingertips. Obviously, there was no way they could. Then I asked them to envision a lakeshore. How many grains of sand are there? How about under the lake water? And what about an ocean beach and the grains of sand that make up the ocean floor? The number is unfathomable. And yet Psalm 139 states that God's thoughts of us *outnumber* the grains of sand.

From the looks on their faces, I could see that my students' minds were blown. And I understood their reaction.

When I was their age—and even throughout college and sometimes as an adult—I never felt like anyone's top friend choice. I never felt truly, fully, wholly known. No friend was finishing my sentences, no friend could seemingly read my mind, no friend wanted to spend every waking hour hanging out or talking on the phone, and no friend could fully understand my feelings. (Note: I realize these are massively high expectations for a school-age or any-age friendship. I blame the copious number of YA novels I read during those years for raising my friendship hopes and dreams.)

As unrealistic as those dreams were, I still have days when it feels like no one really knows me or wants to take the time and energy to get to know who I am. My husband of almost fifteen years is the one who comes closest to knowing me fully. But even with him there are feelings or reactions I need to explain, parts of my personality that surprise even me, and pieces of me that fall apart with little advance notice.

So it's mind-blowing to realize that the Creator of the universe thinks of us nonstop, knows every single intricate detail about us, and yet adores us.

Being known so fully sounds enticing and also a little terrifying. I mean, *fully known* means all the way. Completely. Totally. Every single part. There's a good reason that no person can fully know someone else: it's overwhelming. God is the only one who can know us completely, and thank goodness. He doesn't just see the best, prettiest, and most presentable portions of our selves. God also sees every deep, dark, ugly, secret part, and still He chooses to love us. He sees it all, knows it all, and loves us completely anyway.

Psalm 139 contains so many treasures that can bring calm and joy to our hearts. Because of the truths it lists, we can be empowered to rest in being known. We are knitted together by the One who created the original pattern, the One who chooses us again and again, the One who loves us as we are. We are examined and still adored. What a gift!

LORD, *You have searched me and You know me, and still You love me. Thank You for an indescribable love that embraces all of me as I am. Even when I feel unknown by others, help me to remember that Your knowledge of me is a comfort. May I spend my days living into the strength You offer in being known. Amen.*

REFLECT

Who comes the closest to fully knowing you?

How do the truths in Psalm 139 make you feel?

Empowered to Be Accepted

But God proves his own love for us in that while we were still sinners, Christ died for us.

Romans 5:8 CSB

I remember the day I became a full-fledged perfectionist. I was
five years old, and I was afraid I wouldn't be smart enough to pass
kindergarten.

Sitting in the bathroom while my mom got ready for the day, I pep-
pered her with questions:

Did you ever flunk a grade?
What about Dad? Did he?
What if I do? What then?

All these years later, I can still feel the anxiety that bubbled up in
my little heart as I worried that I wouldn't be able to cut it.

Later that year, my kindergarten class took a test. I don't recall
whether it was a standardized test or just a regular assessment, but
I remember coming to a question I couldn't answer and for the first
time being tempted to look at my neighbor's paper. I was so panicked that I wouldn't answer every question correctly that I considered
cheating—on a kindergarten test.

Looking back at my family and my upbringing, I can see where
some of those anxieties came from. But I'm also certain I was at least

partly born that way. I must have been, because while I was given high standards and expectations, I was also told more times than I could count that I was loved—by my parents and by God.

What my perfectionist heart has always struggled to understand is God's choice to love us—and to act on that love so radically—while we were still sinners. And then, even after we learn about God and ask for His forgiveness, we continue to make mistakes and bad choices, and He continues to accept and love us! Even if we turn away from God completely, He never stops loving us.

And it isn't in a low-key, passive, "Oh yeah, I love that gal" sort of way. No, He loves us with a personal, passionate, "I will die for you" kind of love. Not when we're good enough. Not when we get our act together. Not when we kick the habit or finish the project or earn the medal or go on the mission trip. No, He accepts us as we are *now*.

God could have demanded that we live up to a set of expectations, that we meet a set of standards before He welcomes us into His family. He could have treated us like college applicants or Facebook users trying to join a private group. He could have been as strict as the most severe homeowners association or the most prestigious country club. But instead He welcomes every single one of us just as we are.

We don't have to fill out an application and hope for the best. We don't need to polish our résumés, pump up our qualifications, or provide references. Jesus *is* our reference, and only through Him are we qualified. Because of the work He's done on our behalf, we're in. We are accepted into the family of God without having to meet expectations or earn extra credit.

While we were still sinners, Jesus died for us—and because of that mind-blowing, heart-shattering truth, we are fully accepted by God. *You* are accepted by God.

With such an enormous gift of grace, we can now turn to one another and extend that same grace. If the God of the universe looks at each one of us and says "You're in. You're one of Mine," then how can we possibly hold a higher standard for anyone else? If God says I'm loved and accepted just as I am, then I am—and so are you.

> **LORD**, *it's hard to believe that You see all of me and accept me just as I am. Thank You for Christ who qualifies me. When I forget that He is enough, please help me believe. Help me remember how You've welcomed me into Your family with open arms, and empower me to do the same for others. Thank You, God. Amen.*

REFLECT

How does knowing you are fully accepted by God change how you then treat others?

What's one way you can extend that freely given grace to someone else?

The Power of God's Healing

Luke 13:10–17

On a Sabbath Jesus was teaching in one of the synagogues, and a woman was there who had been crippled by a spirit for eighteen years. She was bent over and could not straighten up at all. When Jesus saw her, he called her forward and said to her, "Woman, you are set free from your infirmity." Then he put his hands on her, and immediately she straightened up and praised God.

Indignant because Jesus had healed on the Sabbath, the synagogue leader said to the people, "There are six days for work. So come and be healed on those days, not on the Sabbath."

The Lord answered him, "You hypocrites! Doesn't each of you on the Sabbath untie your ox or donkey from the stall and lead it out to give it water? Then should not this woman, a daughter of Abraham, whom Satan has kept bound for eighteen long years, be set free on the Sabbath day from what bound her?"

When he said this, all his opponents were humiliated, but the people were delighted with all the wonderful things he was doing.

GOD, *thank You that nothing is impossible with You. I pray for myself and for those in my family and community who are physically struggling and in pain. Please heal them. I trust You. Amen.*

REFLECT

What can we learn about God's perspective of physical healing from this Scripture passage?

What is God inviting you to ask of Him through this story?

Empowered to Be Healthy

Don't you know that your body is a temple of the Holy Spirit who is in you, whom you have from God? You are not your own, for you were bought at a price. So glorify God with your body.

1 Corinthians 6:19–20 CSB

You have restored me to health
and let me live.

Isaiah 38:16 CSB

Several years ago, I woke up ready to restore my body.

I had three of my children in less than four years. I'd spent a total of almost seven years either pregnant, nursing, or both, and my body had wrung itself out. It had expanded and deflated, grown and birthed, fed and nourished, carried, rocked, cradled, and chased. And then one day, I realized that I was not pregnant, nursing, or toddler-chasing exhausted.

My body was in need of restoration, so that day I simply decided to be ready to make choices that would restore it back to health. And eighteen months from that day, I was more than sixty pounds lighter.

No, I never followed a specific diet; I merely made one better choice at a time. One donut instead of three. A small latte instead of a large. Daily walks with my dog, our mileage increasing each day. I took my time with the process, making simple changes that added up. One day and one choice and one baby step at a time. As it turns out, slow and steady really does win the race, which in this case led me back to health.

It was never about losing weight; it was about becoming a healthier version of myself *for* myself. And for me, the journey started with losing weight. To be clear—I wasn't ashamed of my weight. I wasn't a bad person because of those extra pounds or a better person after I lost them, because weight does not equal worth. It was simply where I began.

A couple years later, I was thrilled to be expecting my fourth child. My body would once again take on the role of carrier, vessel, and nurturer. As I adjusted my thoughts to literally make space for growth, it was clear that what I'd gained during the journey far outweighed the sixty pounds that I'd lost.

It felt darn good to be able to move in the way I wanted to. I could walk faster and farther than ever before, sometimes even jogging. I was drinking more water each day than I ever had. I felt healthy, strong, and proud of taking time for self-care.

My kids said I was shrinking, but I knew that, choice by choice, I was growing into who I was meant to be.

Our daily choices can become reflections of who we really are.

I think our health matters to God for two reasons. First, God wants us to care for His creation—and that includes our bodies. We care for our church buildings, our homes, and other spaces where we gather and welcome God's Spirit, right? We spend time cleaning and caring for those spaces, and we deserve the same for ourselves. For me, that looks like eating well and taking daily walks, which in combination led to weight loss. Maybe for you it's moving your body, cleaning out your closet so it only holds clothes that fit right now, or taking a long bath. Whatever brings God glory and lets you truly live.

Second, I find that when I'm intentionally caring for my body, I'm happier and better able to care for (and about) my family and loved ones. When I take care of myself, everyone around me also benefits, and I believe God cares about this too.

God is cheering us on as we care for ourselves in ways that bring Him glory. God delights in our restoration, in our health, and in His people taking good care of themselves in order to glorify Him—which we can do in big and small ways.

Here's to recognizing the strength in small changes and the ways they can impact our health and our lives.

> **LORD**, *thank You for choosing my heart, soul, and body to live in. My health matters to You, and I'm grateful. Help me to take good care of myself, recognizing that I am a temple of the Holy Spirit. Give me strength to make wise daily choices that will have life-giving, long-term effects. Even in this, I look to You. Amen.*

REFLECT

What is one small daily choice you can make right now to take good care of yourself?

What gets in the way of your actual self-care?

Empowered to Be Confident

For we are God's masterpiece. He has created us anew in Christ Jesus, so we can do the good things he planned for us long ago.

Ephesians 2:10 NLT

I sat on the edge of my seat and listened as the deacon gave announcements. My mind was going a million miles a minute trying to think of a way for this to end well, but I couldn't see it. The pit of my stomach felt heavy. It was the same feeling I get at the top of a roller coaster, when the anticipation is at its peak and I don't know if the drop will be exhilarating or excruciating (mostly excruciating). And that was when I noticed the deacon looking in my direction and heard him saying, "Let's welcome Pastor Grace as she gives the message for us today!"

I had been at the church about six months as the newest associate pastor. I was fresh out of seminary with a master's degree in world missions but hadn't made it to the mission field as I had imagined I would. I had never taken a preaching class, but here I was about to take the mic and preach my first sermon.

I wiped my palms down the sides of my skinny jeans, but it didn't help. I walked to the music stand, laid open my trusty NIV Bible, and proceeded to read Scripture passages for the next twenty minutes, hoping that would be enough to carry the message.

It was embarrassing, a failure—and it happened to be Easter Sunday.

I still cringe when I think about that moment. It's so deeply imprinted on my memory that now anytime I'm asked to speak or preach, it's the first thing that comes to mind. And along with it I hear this half-truth: *Who do you think you are? You're not qualified. You don't have enough experience. You need more training or education to be considered a professional.*

I listen to the critic's voice in my head as if she's full of wisdom and care for me. It's easy to understand her logic and to think she's only trying to spare me from more shame. What she says is partially true: I wasn't taught to be a preacher. I've never taken courses about how to become an excellent speaker. I've read some books and listened to some TED talks, but that's not enough to be considered a professional.

But the critic's half-truth goes further: *If you can't be a professional, what are you doing? Let others who are more eloquent and knowledgeable do the work of preaching and teaching.*

I wrestle these thoughts to their core message, and the lie becomes clear: *You aren't good enough, and you never will be.*

The words hurt me where I'm tender. I'm nearly convinced that the lies are true when I remember how many times I've heard from God that I am to use my words to lead. He has made that abundantly clear. But in my humanness and doubt, I ask Him one more time, *Lord, are You sure?*

I sense God lovingly reply, *Who are you to say whether My word is true or not? Am I not the One who created the world and who, even before then, thought of you and all that you would be? Whose voice will you listen to?*

He knows I know the answer. I'm His masterpiece, but I've counted myself as the one who didn't make the cut. Because He is the Artist who created me, He knows every stroke of paint, every layered texture, every hidden gift that will unfold as I trust Him and say yes to Him.

So even though my knees still shake and the critic's voice still whispers lies, the next time I'm asked to speak I step up to the podium, hold the mic, and let His words tell the truth.

LORD, *I am Your masterpiece. Even as I say it, I need faith to believe it more. Thank You for the good things You've planned for my life from before the beginning of time. When I feel inadequate to step into those good things, I pray that You would be my confidence and that Your word to me would be the most important qualification I need. Thank You that I can stand tall and firm because You are in me. Amen.*

REFLECT

What lies do you hear from the critics—whether that's the critic inside your head or the people around you?

What are the truths God is telling you in response to those lies?

The Power of Singing

Exodus 15:19–21

When Pharaoh's horses with his chariots and horsemen went into the sea, the LORD brought the water of the sea back over them. But the Israelites walked through the sea on dry ground. Then the prophetess Miriam, Aaron's sister, took a tambourine in her hand, and all the women came out following her with tambourines and dancing. Miriam sang to them:

> Sing to the LORD,
> for he is highly exalted;
> he has thrown the horse
> and its rider into the sea. (CSB)

GOD, *in victory or in difficulty, let my singing remind me of Your power and presence. Amen.*

REFLECT

What can you learn about the power of song through this passage?

What is a song you can sing in response to what God is doing in your life?

Empowered to Be Resilient

And not only that, but we also boast in our afflictions, because we know that affliction produces endurance, endurance produces proven character, and proven character produces hope. This hope will not disappoint us, because God's love has been poured out in our hearts through the Holy Spirit who was given to us.

Romans 5:3–5 CSB

Grief lies like a foot of floodwater in our home. I'm not wading through it all the time, but when I hear of another death—due to illness, due to police brutality, due to depression—the waters rise, and it feels as though I can't tread water long enough to keep myself afloat.

It's not only loss of life that keeps me trudging through grief. It's the daily reminders that Black bodies are not safe doing everyday things, that xenophobia continues to feed anti-Asian racism, that the disparity between the rich and poor becomes wider, that there are children forever separated from their parents at the border. Grief mingles with wrath and lament and hopelessness, and I don't have the energy to envision what life could be like in the future.

And even within the walls of our home and in our close friendships, we're facing unexpected illnesses, deep wounds in marriage, and the tensions of caring for young children and aging parents.

Twice last week, I cried myself to sleep. I couldn't pinpoint exactly what was wrong, which only added frustration to the restlessness I already felt. Every night, I try to push anxiety to the edges of my mind, but it shows up center stage when my body finally relents and lets me sleep. Instead of rest, anxiety turns sleep into hours of vivid dreams that keep my mind unsettled.

I've become slow at processing information. I listen to people talk and I try to keep up with the news, but my brain only seems to catch half of it—if that.

Each loss, each death, each painful memory of a wound that hasn't properly healed feels like a wave crashing over my head. Its powerful current keeps me under, and I become disoriented, desperate to be pulled out and set on dry land.

How do we keep going when life resists us from doing so? How do we endure hard things when we're being pummeled left and right?

Perseverance and hope seem wonderful when we consider them from a distance. We know they're essential to faith, but when we're drowning, they seem irrelevant, even cruel. *Perseverance* sounds like gritting our teeth and clenching our fists until the difficulty passes, while *hope* sounds like a flighty, feel-good word that doesn't hold weight in suffering.

I wrestle with God about these two words, thrashing in my grief yet unwilling to let go until I understand. And in return, He gives me a new word: *resilience*.

He reminds me that "faith shows the reality of what we hope for; it is the evidence of things we cannot see" (Heb. 11:1 NLT). And from there, the stories of old come to mind—of Noah and Abraham, of Moses and Rahab, of the many saints who have died, whether in glory or obscurity. He reminds me of my grandmother, who was widowed at a young age and raised her three children as a single mother, and of my husband's grandfather, who lived and fought through poverty and wartimes.

They had resilience through faith *because* they had to persevere through hard things. It wasn't by white-knuckling through the years of suffering but by trusting in God who holds all of eternity in His hands. Their hope wasn't in what they could tangibly grasp. Their hope was Christ Himself, who endured it all—even death.

Perseverance is the path to hope, and hope will not disappoint us. It is what fuels us to endure and makes us resilient to face whatever comes our way.

And we are not alone in this. We are surrounded by a huge crowd of witnesses who have gone before us (Heb. 12:1). And Christ, who persevered through all things, is with us. We can look to Him to anchor us in hope no matter how much the waters rise.

LORD, *thank You that the hope I have in You doesn't disappoint. Thank You for the many saints who have gone before me, whose lives are testimonies that You are faithful and able to make me resilient and tenacious. Help me to keep going. Turn my face toward You to look for hope. Amen.*

REFLECT

How is God teaching you resilience in the season of life you're in now?

How are you holding on to hope when life is overwhelming?

Empowered to Be a Friend

A friend loves at all times, and a brother is born for a difficult time.

Proverbs 17:17 CSB

One of my best friends texted me and asked if I wanted to get together. She knew a place with a patio, and the cooler weather made it the perfect time to catch up over a cup of coffee. Her invitation took me by surprise, and I realized it had been a while since I had met a friend just for fun.

Over the several weeks prior to this coffee date, I had messaged and talked to and even visited in person with several friends. But very few of those connections involved anything lighthearted or laid-back. Game nights and barbecues felt like a distant memory, and I knew at least a year had passed since my last happy hour with girlfriends.

Instead, I'd sent a gift card for food delivery to a friend whose husband had been diagnosed with cancer. I'd taken my daughter to a friend's salon to repair the mess left after my girl attempted to cut her own hair. I'd driven a friend to the police station to file a report against her abusive ex-husband. I'd also opened a card full of encouraging words from a fellow mom in the trenches of stressful everyday life, and I'd sent a note to another friend's dad who was living alone in a nursing home. In my planner I'd written the dates of friends' scary medical appointments, and I'd sent a short-notice SOS to a friend, asking her to babysit my youngest daughter while I met a deadline.

When my friend Kate said, "Hey, let's get coffee!" (and neither one of us had an agenda or a pressing need outside of catching up), I realized how many hard roads my friends and I had been walking together. We'd all been in a dark season, and it showed—but not in the way you might guess. Though I missed late-night laughter and spontaneous socializing, I wasn't sorry my recent interactions with friends were more serious ones. Instead, I was thankful.

When life gets hard, it's not uncommon for friendships to fade away, for relationships to take a backseat to crisis management, for those we were once closest with to keep their distance. Sometimes it happens because we push people away; sometimes it's just easier to hunker down and try to handle life on our own.

The Bible gives us example after example, though, of how God created us to be interconnected and interdependent. Paul gives us the illustration of the church being like a body, where all the parts are necessary and unique and work together (1 Cor. 12:12–26). Though it's possible to function without a hand or an eye, it's not optimal. Likewise, we can usually survive without friends, but rarely do we thrive without at least one or two people to lean on, laugh with, and love.

Are you facing something difficult right now? Or is someone you love going through a hard time? Don't give in to the temptation to pull back. Don't let the world tell you—or your friend—that it's smarter or stronger or safer to face challenges alone. Instead, listen to what Scripture says about encouraging one another (1 Thess. 5:11) and bearing one another's burdens (Gal. 6:2). Follow the examples of Moses, who let Aaron and Hur hold up his arms when he got tired (Exod. 17:10–13); of Ruth and Naomi, who together faced their grief and their lives as widows; of the disciples, who started churches and spread the good news of Jesus together.

Allow the Holy Spirit to give you the courage to reach out when you're hurting or to reach out to someone else in pain. Allow Him to increase your capacity for compassion and your ability to empathize. Ask Him to help you be a friend who loves at all times.

GOD, *thank You for the friends You've placed in my life. Even though I sometimes feel like it's safer to face life alone, I know You've created us for community in both the fun and the hard parts of life. Please give me the courage to reach out to someone this week, and give me a heart of welcome and warmth when others are brave enough to reach out to me. In Jesus's name, amen.*

REFLECT

Who can you connect with or reach out to this week?

When are you tempted to pull back in your friendships?

The Power of Being in the Right Place at the Right Time

Joshua 2:1–24

Then Joshua son of Nun secretly sent two spies from Shittim. "Go, look over the land," he said, "especially Jericho." So they went and entered the house of a prostitute named Rahab and stayed there. The king of Jericho was told, "Look, some of the Israelites have come here tonight to spy out the land." So the king of Jericho sent this message to Rahab: "Bring out the men who came to you and entered your house, because they have come to spy out the whole land."

But the woman had taken the two men and hidden them. She said, "Yes, the men came to me, but I did not know where they had come from. At dusk, when it was time to close the city gate, they left. I don't know which way they went. Go after them quickly. You may catch up with them." (But she had taken them up to the roof and hidden them under the stalks of flax she had laid out on the roof.) So the men set out in pursuit of the spies on the road that leads to the fords of the Jordan, and as soon as the pursuers had gone out, the gate was shut.

Before the spies lay down for the night, she went up on the roof and said to them, "I know that the LORD has given you this land and that a great fear of you has fallen on us, so that all who live in this country are melting in fear because of you. We have heard how the LORD dried up the water of the Red Sea for you when you came out of Egypt, and what you did to Sihon and Og, the two kings of the Amorites east of the Jordan, whom you completely destroyed. When we heard of it, our hearts melted in fear and everyone's courage failed because of you, for the Lᴏʀᴅ your God is God in heaven above and on the earth below.

"Now then, please swear to me by the Lᴏʀᴅ that you will show kindness to my family, because I have shown kindness to you. Give me a sure sign that you will spare the lives of my father and mother, my brothers and sisters, and all who belong to them—and that you will save us from death."

"Our lives for your lives!" the men assured her. "If you don't tell what we are doing, we will treat you kindly and faithfully when the Lᴏʀᴅ gives us the land."

So she let them down by a rope through the window, for the house she lived in was part of the city wall. She said to them, "Go to the hills so the pursuers will not find you. Hide yourselves there three days until they return, and then go on your way."

Now the men had said to her, "This oath you made us swear will not be binding on us unless, when we enter the land, you have tied this scarlet cord in the window through which you let us down, and unless you have brought your father and mother, your brothers and all your family into your house. If any of them go outside your house into the street, their blood will be on their own heads; we will not be responsible. As for those who are in the house with you, their blood will be on our head if a hand is laid on them. But if you tell what we are doing, we will be released from the oath you made us swear."

"Agreed," she replied. "Let it be as you say."

So she sent them away, and they departed. And she tied the scarlet cord in the window.

When they left, they went into the hills and stayed there three days, until the pursuers had searched all along the road and returned without finding them. Then the two men started back. They went down out of the hills, forded the river and came to Joshua son of Nun and told him everything that had happened to them. They said to Joshua, "The Lᴏʀᴅ has surely given the whole land into our hands; all the people are melting in fear because of us."

GOD, *wherever I am, whatever I'm doing, I'm here to do Your will. Amen.*

REFLECT

What can you learn about God through the story of Rahab?

What is God saying to you about the power of being in the right place at the right time?

Empowered to Be Quenched by Living Water

A woman of Samaria came to draw water.

"Give me a drink," Jesus said to her, because his disciples had gone into town to buy food.

"How is it that you, a Jew, ask for a drink from me, a Samaritan woman?" she asked him. For Jews do not associate with Samaritans.

Jesus answered, "If you knew the gift of God, and who is saying to you, 'Give me a drink,' you would ask him, and he would give you living water."

"Sir," said the woman, "you don't even have a bucket, and the well is deep. So where do you get this 'living water'? You aren't greater than our father Jacob, are you? He gave us the well and drank from it himself, as did his sons and livestock."

Jesus said, "Everyone who drinks from this water will get thirsty again. But whoever drinks from the water that I will give him will never get thirsty again. In fact, the water I will give him will become a well of water springing up in him for eternal life."

"Sir," the woman said to him, "give me this water so that I won't get thirsty and come here to draw water."

John 4:7–15 CSB

In the not-so-distant past, I was in a season of survival mode. I was pregnant with my fourth child and found myself constantly on the couch, sick and exhausted. COVID-19 had taken over the news and our lives. I was schooling my three elementary-age kids from home, while my husband and I both worked from home. My porch became a one-room schoolhouse. There were more meals and snacks and fingerprints and spills and time together than ever. My dishwasher was running continuously, and I realized that I hadn't left the house by myself in weeks.

I had reached new levels of sloth. My water intake and nutrition were shot. I wasn't taking my usual daily walks. My sleep was interrupted and short, and so was my temper. I'm a planner, but a blank calendar and no end in sight was wreaking havoc on my brain and heart.

I was getting by, scraping the bottom of my self-care barrel.

I needed to focus on meeting my basic needs. Rest. Water. Good food. Walking. Brushing my teeth. Meal planning. One load of laundry at a time. Reading books instead of endless, mind-numbing scrolling. *Basics.*

That's what I needed. As I began trying to meet my basic needs, I found that reviving them can change a life, right things that are upended, and allow space for growth. I learned that fueling our tanks with genuine self-care can lead to filling others with hope, peace, and joy. I realized that the basics are not big things, just one little thing at a time, and that's what makes them possible.

But the most important thing I'm still discovering is that God meets us in the basics.

When we thirst, it's water that quenches. When we hunger, it's bread that fills. When we're lonely and tired and overwhelmed, it's love that revives our hearts.

Sometimes the basics can be unattainable. There are seasons of life when we are not able to meet certain needs, such as while parenting a newborn. Sleep? Routine? Not likely. But when I am able to get enough sleep and water and not do a whole lot of social-media scrolling, I feel refreshed, renewed, and ready for the day.

And if ounces of water can do that for our bodies, imagine what a deep drink of living water can do for our souls.

The story of Jesus meeting a Samaritan woman at a well is one of my favorites. Jesus meets her right in the midst of her messy life and offers her His love, His living water. And after she gets a taste, she runs off to tell her whole city, becoming quite the unlikely evangelist.

No matter where God meets us or how dry our souls may be, that living water can revive like nothing else. And when we tell others the story of who we've become after drinking deeply, of where God met us and the truths He told us about ourselves, eternities change.

Jesus can change water into wine (John 2:1–11), and He can transform water-fetchers into missionaries. When our basic needs are met, we can be ready for Him to get all up in our business, making changes in a living-water kind of way.

We never know how Jesus will show up in our messes, ready to change our regular water into living water. But when He does, He'll bring revival and refreshment to our hearts and lives.

WITH EVERY SIP OF WATER I TAKE TODAY, *Lord,*

meet me right where I am. I'm thirsting for You, for the living water only You can provide. May it fill the cracks in my dry and weary heart, overflowing into my thoughts and actions as I go about this day. Thank You for meeting each of us at our own well. Amen.

REFLECT

What basics have been running low for you that can be revived?

How has Jesus met you with living water, bringing refreshment into your life?

Empowered to Be at Peace

He reached down from on high and took hold of me;
he drew me out of deep waters.
He rescued me from my powerful enemy,
from my foes, who were too strong for me.
They confronted me in the day of my disaster,
but the LORD was my support.
He brought me out into a spacious place;
he rescued me because he delighted in me.

Psalm 18:16–19

We welcome 2020 as we usually do for New Year's Day—a lunch-to-dinner gathering at the grandparents' house. Seventeen of us pack into their two-bedroom retirement home, and the air is abuzz and fragrant. Great-grandchildren find trinkets around the house to play with, their energy too high for any of the adults to handle. The moms and aunts busy themselves with the cooking and make sure everyone has a preview bite of what's to come. The dads and uncles chat and keep the grandparents company.

It's a typical beginning to the year, and in our bliss, we are unaware of what is to come.

By February, we hear murmurs of COVID-19 spreading around the world, but we feel untouchable in the US, safe and at peace while the world scrambles. But by March, we're on lockdown. Fear binds us up in stress and anxiety, and we watch how sorely unprepared we are as a nation to deal with the many, many people who get sick from the disease and who die from it. Hospitals set up makeshift tents to care for patients, and morgues fill up too quickly. Mortuaries and cemeteries are backed up, and those who grieve must wait longer to bury their dead. There is just no more room.

Our kids stop going to school and start distance learning. They are disoriented and grieve alongside us, and we don't have any answers for all their questions.

By April, we start to hear about friends of friends getting sick, and soon enough it hits our church community. Every day our kids pray, "God, please make coronavirus go away," and we respond with amens, hoping it really does disappear, though the panic sets in.

I start to feel unsafe going out to get gas or to Costco after hearing about an Asian American family whose faces were slashed inside a Sam's Club in Texas. They were being blamed for the virus because of their ethnicity. Anti-Asian racism continues to rise, and I'm afraid for my children, for my husband, and for myself anytime we have to leave the house.

In May, George Floyd is murdered at the hands of police officers, and the world can see how racism is alive and well in our country. He is only one of many Black men and women whose names become a cry for justice. There is no peace when there is no justice, and I search the Psalms for words to pray against the powers that keep systems of oppression in place. I ask God to bring down the wicked, to intervene.

All the while, work doesn't slow down and deadlines loom over me like dark clouds that threaten to drown me if I don't meet them. The problem is I'm *already* drowning, and still there is more pain to come. Peace now feels like a distant dream that won't come true.

In June, our grandpa passes away, and in July, a church member dies of COVID-19.

No more, I beg God. *Please, please just make it all stop.*

The waters are too deep, the waves too strong. Everything is pushing me further down. When I pause for a moment and take in all that has transpired, I notice my breaths become shallow. My chest tightens. I become overwhelmed by all the heartache.

What is peace at a time like this? I wrestle with my reality, and deep down I know that true peace can be found even now—but only when I'm tethered to God. He is the one steady Person I can fully rely on and the One who understands the anguish of humanity. He knows what it feels like to lose loved ones to death, to be surrounded by people who come after your humanity, and to be betrayed in friendship. He overcame death and was raised to life with a glorified body that still bears His scars.

If He bore it all, surely the peace He offers is real because He embodies it in Himself. I ask God for space to breathe, and He brings to mind my favorite image of peace: a vast meadow where a breeze makes the tall grass sway. I imagine myself standing in the middle of it and take deep breaths. His presence is peace. The Holy Spirit soothes and comforts my soul, and I find my footing again.

GOD OF PEACE, *I need You. I have no control over what's happening in my life, and I'm overwhelmed by it all. Only You can help me stay grounded. Holy Spirit, anchor me to Yourself and steady me. In Jesus's name, amen.*

REFLECT

What practices or images help you find peace in the midst of chaos?

How does being aware of God's presence calm your spirit?

The Power of God's Voice in Our Rage

Mark 4:35–41

That day when evening came, he said to his disciples, "Let us go over to the other side." Leaving the crowd behind, they took him along, just as he was, in the boat. There were also other boats with him. A furious squall came up, and the waves broke over the boat, so that it was nearly swamped. Jesus was in the stern, sleeping on a cushion. The disciples woke him and said to him, "Teacher, don't you care if we drown?"

He got up, rebuked the wind and said to the waves, "Quiet! Be still!" Then the wind died down and it was completely calm.

He said to his disciples, "Why are you so afraid? Do you still have no faith?"

They were terrified and asked each other, "Who is this? Even the wind and the waves obey him!"

> **GOD**, *thank You that in Your presence is peace, even when everything is raging inside and around me. Still the storms inside my soul. Amen.*

REFLECT

What can you learn about how God views our range of emotions through this passage?

What is God saying to you if you're in the midst of an emotional storm?

Empowered to Be Named

Indeed, the hairs of your head are all counted. Don't be afraid; you
are worth more than many sparrows.

Luke 12:7 CSB

When I was in high school, my friend and I had a running joke. We
would pretend to call the boys we liked and begin the phone conversation like this: "Hi, this is Mary . . . Walters . . . from school? . . . your
school? . . . We have three classes together? . . ."

Our assumption was that we were insignificant or even invisible.
Though we made a joke of it, we truly believed we were such no-
bodies, we were so unimportant, that even someone we cared about
would not recognize our voices or even our names. It was a silly gag,
especially considering the small size of our school, but it reflected our
serious insecurities and anxieties. I see now how it made clear our
deep desire to be known.

I wish I could say that fear has disappeared over the decades, but it
hasn't. Just yesterday I texted someone I'd already corresponded with
several times and still started my message by saying, "This is Mary
Carver." I end my emails to my kids' teachers or their friends' parents
with "Mary, Adrienne's [or Annalyn's] mom." I make sure to include
my maiden name on my Facebook profile so that no matter when a
person knew me, they'll recognize and remember me. And when it
comes to my work? I'm constantly clarifying my qualifications with
lists of successful and well-known people I've worked with over the

years—as if I can be considered capable or trustworthy only through association with someone else's name.

These habits could be explained away as necessary in a world where we're way too connected and know way too many people. Who could be expected to remember my name when they have 983 so-called friends on Facebook? I could explain my constant résumé references as a savvy business move—and besides, everyone does it. Everyone name-drops in order to promote themselves. But when I'm honest, when I'm quiet and I sit with the Lord and listen, I know the truth.

The truth is that I forget what matters. I forget who it is I really want to know my name. I forget that God has named me. He calls me daughter and beloved and forgiven—and that's what matters.

It doesn't matter if an acquaintance from school or work or my old church or the PTA forgets my name. The God of the universe knows my name. He knows me! And He knows you too.

God knows us so well that He reminds us of this truth over and over. He knows we're going to forget. He knows we're going to get turned around and upside down about who and what matters. He knows we need constant reassurance that we matter to Him.

We find these reminders in the Old Testament, where God says, "Do not fear . . . I have called you by your name; you are mine" (Isa. 43:1 CSB). We find them in the New Testament too. In the book of Luke, Jesus says that God knows us so well, He has even counted the number of hairs on our head (Luke 12:7). In the book of John, Jesus tells His followers, "I know my own, and my own know me" (John 10:14 CSB).

We don't need to worry about someone forgetting our name or not knowing it in the first place. We don't need to work overtime to prove ourselves and our worth. We don't need to fear insignificance or irrelevance. The God of the universe has called us by name. He has called us His beloved children.

If you feel unnoticed or anonymous, remember that you have been created and named by God. Allow Him to give you holy confidence in who you are as you live out the purpose He's given you. Stand tall in the truth that you belong to Him and He knows your name.

OH GOD, *thank You for knowing me so well. Thank You for calling me by name. I'm so humbled by that! Please keep me mindful of Your love and Your care for me, and help me remember that being known by You is more important than credit or recognition by anyone else. In Jesus's name, amen.*

REFLECT

How does believing that God knows you and calls you by name change the way you see yourself?

How can you offer that same gift to someone else?

Empowered to Be Extravagant in Love

Meanwhile, Jesus was in Bethany at the home of Simon, a man who had previously had leprosy. While he was eating, a woman came in with a beautiful alabaster jar of expensive perfume made from essence of nard. She broke open the jar and poured the perfume over his head.

Some of those at the table were indignant. "Why waste such expensive perfume?" they asked. "It could have been sold for a year's wages and the money given to the poor!" So they scolded her harshly.

But Jesus replied, "Leave her alone. Why criticize her for doing such a good thing to me? You will always have the poor among you, and you can help them whenever you want to. But you will not always have me. She has done what she could and has anointed my body for burial ahead of time. I tell you the truth, wherever the Good News is preached throughout the world, this woman's deed will be remembered and discussed."

Mark 14:3–9 NLT

As a woman and as a mom, I constantly pour out love without expecting anything in return. Since my kids were babies, I've given up my body for their benefit. I nursed them, spending every waking hour (and many of the non-waking ones) feeding them, changing their diapers, doing their laundry, and bouncing or rocking them. I've made grilled cheese sandwiches, tied shoes, prayed over consequences, and stayed up into the wee hours listening and worrying and picking up the house. I've done most of this while wearing the previous day's clothes that I picked up off the floor, and very likely without having eaten a hot or complete meal myself that day.

As a daughter, as a wife, and as a friend, I've also been on the receiving end of such love.

My mom, a single mother from the time my siblings and I were very young, burned the candle at both ends to provide for us. Now that we are adults, she continues to love and care for us in new ways. One time she drove ten hours to watch my baby daughter while I participated in a work retreat, and she told me she loved every minute.

My husband pours out his love in both big and small ways. The dishes are his domain, and for that I am so thankful. (I love to cook. The cleanup? Not so much.) He makes sure my water bottle is full at night and my mug of coffee is poured in the morning. He cheers me on through countless work projects, holds my hand during scary dental procedures, and folds all the laundry.

Over the years my friends have shown up at different times to love me well. They have scrubbed my toilets. Cooked and dropped off meals. Prayed over text messages. Laughed and cried through both fun and hard times.

Love often calls for sacrificing our own comfort. We see this kind of extravagant love poured out in our own lives, we see this in the life of Christ, and we see it in Mark 14.

Jesus was eating a meal, and a woman came ready to pour out her love. Can you imagine the hammering of her heart as she approached the table? Can you see the look of hope, adoration, and terror on her face as she offered her lavish gift? Can you imagine Jesus looking at her with love and acceptance?

And then the disciples had the nerve to ridicule her offering. I love the way Jesus rebukes them, saying her gift would be remembered. What a comeback!

That woman recognized the extravagant love Jesus offered, and expecting nothing in return, she lavishly poured out her own love on Him. We too can give extravagantly of ourselves.

We can love our families by returning home to continue our work after a long day on the job. We can clean bathrooms, cook meals, and go back to the office the next day. We can wipe baby bottoms in the middle of the night or stroke a middle schooler's hair after they've had a hard day. We can switch loads of laundry and do the dishes for the fifth time that day. All are gifts we give—some to ourselves and some to others—but are likely never thanked for.

Some of the most fulfilling gifts we can give are anonymous, and therefore thanks-less. There's something heart-swelling about giving to someone without the possibility of being thanked, recognized, or credited. Maybe it's paying for a stranger's coffee order in the drive-through or leaving a small gift or card on a friend's doorstep. These acts are quiet in their anonymity, and heartfelt for both giver and recipient.

Jesus loved us extravagantly to the end, pouring out His own life so that we may live fully, abundantly (John 10:10). Because of the extravagant way we have been loved by Christ, we can do the hard work of daily living. And just as the woman poured out her heart and soul for Jesus with a jar of perfume, we can do the same for our family, friends, selves, and God.

LORD, *thank You for going first in showing me how to love extravagantly. May I learn from You and then turn to those around me and do likewise. I pray that like the woman who poured perfume on Jesus's head, I would pour out to others generously. Amen.*

REFLECT

How can or do you love extravagantly?

In what ways can you give of yourself in love?

The Power of Being Free from Condemnation

John 8:2–11

At dawn [Jesus] appeared again in the temple courts, where all the people gathered around him, and he sat down to teach them. The teachers of the law and the Pharisees brought in a woman caught in adultery. They made her stand before the group and said to Jesus, "Teacher, this woman was caught in the act of adultery. In the Law Moses commanded us to stone such women. Now what do you say?" They were using this question as a trap, in order to have a basis for accusing him.

But Jesus bent down and started to write on the ground with his finger. When they kept on questioning him, he straightened up and said to them, "Let any one of you who is without sin be the first to throw a stone at her." Again he stooped down and wrote on the ground.

At this, those who heard began to go away one at a time, the older ones first, until only Jesus was left, with the woman still standing there. Jesus straightened up and asked her, "Woman, where are they? Has no one condemned you?"

"No one, sir," she said.

"Then neither do I condemn you," Jesus declared. "Go now and leave your life of sin."

GOD, *thank You for Your love that protects me when others try to condemn me. Teach me to walk in freedom and forgiveness. Amen.*

▌REFLECT

What can you learn through this passage about how God offers freedom from sin?

What is God saying to you about the condemnation you might feel from others—or from yourself?

Empowered to Say No

Very early in the morning, while it was still dark, Jesus got up, left the house and went off to a solitary place, where he prayed. Simon and his companions went to look for him, and when they found him, they exclaimed: "Everyone is looking for you!"

Jesus replied, "Let us go somewhere else—to the nearby villages—so I can preach there also. That is why I have come."

Mark 1:35–38

I wash the rice robotically as my mind zigzags between every worry and concern and my increasing to-do list. The braised beef ribs stew in the Dutch oven on the stove, and the aroma of soy sauce, garlic, onions, and ginger fills the kitchen with the smells of home.

I taste the sauce for the beef ribs, and though I've made this dish a dozen times before, I still get nervous when I'm making it for a new mama. I want it to be perfect—for her to experience a mother's love when her own is far away. I was a new mom once with no family close by, so now I want to show up whenever I'm able and provide what I never had. And though my life was overflowing with obligations, I signed up for the meal train anyway.

I pour the rice into the rice cooker, use my index finger to measure the correct amount of water, and I'm amused that somehow it's accurate every single time. I press the cook button to get it going, and as I turn my attention to the next dish I've promised to make, my phone buzzes. I miss the call just as I reach for it and see that a friend has called me twice already.

It must be an emergency. Why else would she be calling me so many times?

I dial her number, and every possible scenario flashes through my head while I wait for her to answer.

"Hi!"

Her chipper greeting dispels all worries, but before I can tell her that I'm busy, she chatters on about her day, how it's been at work lately, her complaints about this and that person, and how exhausted she's been. I watch the minutes pass as I try to stir and juggle the phone and make sure I'm on schedule to get the meal delivered to the new mama on time. I don't know how to get off the phone without seeming rude, so I say nothing but the occasional "yeah" to let her know I'm still listening.

By the time dinner is dropped off and I'm driving home in the quiet of my car, I realize how spent I am. I can feel the whining coming up through my heart to my mind, annoyed at no one specific but taking it out on the slow driver in front of me and . . . myself.

I've passed my limit of pouring out, and I knew it was coming. I probably even knew it when I first signed up to provide a meal, but I have such a hard time saying no. I don't want to be thought of as unfriendly or as someone who doesn't show up. I want people to know that I'm trustworthy and dependable, that I see them and can carry their burdens with them. The problem is that I want to do that for everyone. It seems like the thing Jesus would've done—isn't He the one who sacrificed it all for us?

But when I look closely at His life, I see that He didn't do everything for everyone. He wasn't always available. He made choices, saying yes to some and no to many. In Mark 1:35–38, Jesus's disciples find Him and exclaim, "Everyone is looking for you!" People are clamoring for Him to heal them and to cast demons out of their loved ones. Everyone needs and wants something from Jesus.

But Jesus responds by saying, "Let's go somewhere else." He knows not only His purpose but also His capacity.

He demonstrates this so many times in His life, establishing boundaries with unhealthy people, setting new standards for unsustainable patterns, and upending unjust practices. He retreats to solitary places to pray (Mark 1:35–38). He takes His time and rests when needed, even in the midst of a storm (Mark 4:35–41). He overturns tables in the temple—a hard *no* to those exploiting the poor (John 2:13–16).

Saying no actually *is* being like Jesus. He knew the wisdom of setting boundaries, and He empowers us to do the same. When we are being pulled in every direction, we can say yes to His purpose within our capacity.

LORD, *You don't require us to do all the things all the time. Help me not to get the needs of others confused with what You're asking me to do. Give me the courage and ability to say no, to establish boundaries with those who often cross them, and to see my limitedness as a good thing and not a selfish thing. Amen.*

REFLECT

In what areas of your life do you need to build healthy boundaries?

What's one *no* you're going to say today?

Empowered to Be Patient

Anna, a prophet, was also there in the Temple. She was the daughter of Phanuel from the tribe of Asher, and she was very old. Her husband died when they had been married only seven years. Then she lived as a widow to the age of eighty-four. She never left the Temple but stayed there day and night, worshiping God with fasting and prayer. She came along just as Simeon was talking with Mary and Joseph, and she began praising God. She talked about the child to everyone who had been waiting expectantly for God to rescue Jerusalem.

Luke 2:36–38 NLT

I've spent many years as a member of Weight Watchers, trying and hoping to change my habits and make healthier choices. Nearly every leader I've ever had in the program has counseled new members against impatience, warning us that weight loss—and even more so, life change—takes time. They reminded us that we didn't get to where we were overnight, and it wouldn't change overnight either.

This was the hardest part of my weight-loss journey—harder even than avoiding second helpings at dinner, adding more vegetables to my day, or getting back on the treadmill. Remembering that my problems had developed one day at a time, one pound at a time, even one choice at a time felt impossible when I was finally ready for change and anxious to see results.

Honestly, I've noticed this impatience show up in many areas of my life. Why wait for five to seven business days when I can get my packages with two-day shipping instead? Why let my dinner simmer all day in the slow cooker when I can zap it with the pressure cooker? Why begin watching a television show when it first premieres, waiting a whole week for a new episode, when after a few months I can binge the whole thing on a streaming service? And speaking of streaming, why isn't the latest season of my favorite show available yet?

Like a little kid counting down to a birthday, holiday, or other big event—asking each morning how many more sleeps until the big day—I want what I want, and I want it right now. Whether we're talking about something inconsequential like a television show or something significant like healing or rescue from a serious situation, most of us tend to quickly turn to frustration or even despair when we don't get the answer, the results, or the relief we desire. In a society focused on immediate gratification, we forget the virtue of patience.

Of course, if we're willing, we don't have to look far to see how many good things come only after waiting. Flowers bloom in the spring, but not until they're good and ready. Crops planted in springtime can't be harvested until the summer and fall. We can check on that tomato plant on the back porch every thirty minutes after planting it, but nothing we do will make it produce fruit any faster. If we're patient, though, we might learn to enjoy the process—the watering, the watching, even the waiting for the payoff in the end.

The same is true of God and His plans. We can't make Him move any faster. But if we can learn to be still and wait for the Lord, eventually we will see Him answer our prayers, and in the interim we will discover so much about ourselves and about God. We can grow closer to Him in those seasons of waiting and see our faith deepen as we rely on Him and His good plans.

When I think of Anna in the temple, faithful and patient as she waited for the promised Messiah, I'm inspired to trust God to give me the patience I need in my own life. I laugh when I imagine Anna's joy at seeing Mary and Joseph walk through the doors with Jesus, and I'm encouraged to wait for my own moment to exclaim, "Finally! He's here!" But I can't do it on my own, and, I suspect, neither can you.

Patience does not come naturally for most of us, especially when overnight shipping and thirty-minute delivery are everyday options. But God promises to give us what we need, and that includes patience. As we face long-term challenges and seemingly unending struggles—or even when we simply can't get exactly what we want right when we want it—let's ask God to give us patience. Let's ask Him to empower us to wait for Him like Anna did until the day we see His promises fulfilled.

GOD, *it's so hard to wait. Please help me be patient. Remind me of Your promises and give me faith that You will fulfill them. When impatience rises in me, empower me to wait on You, and help me pay attention to how You move even in the waiting. Amen.*

REFLECT

What are you waiting for today?

How would patience make your wait feel different?

The Power of Being a Woman Leader

Judges 4:4–16

Deborah, a prophetess and the wife of Lappidoth, was judging Israel at that time. She would sit under the palm tree of Deborah between Ramah and Bethel in the hill country of Ephraim, and the Israelites went up to her to settle disputes.

She summoned Barak son of Abinoam from Kedesh in Naphtali and said to him, "Hasn't the Lord, the God of Israel, commanded you, 'Go, deploy the troops on Mount Tabor, and take with you ten thousand men from the Naphtalites and Zebulunites? Then I will lure Sisera commander of Jabin's army, his chariots, and his infantry at the Wadi Kishon to fight against you, and I will hand him over to you.'"

Barak said to her, "If you will go with me, I will go. But if you will not go with me, I will not go."

"I will gladly go with you," she said, "but you will receive no honor on the road you are about to take, because the Lord will sell Sisera to a woman." So Deborah got up and went with Barak to Kedesh. Barak summoned Zebulun and Naphtali to Kedesh; ten thousand men followed him, and Deborah also went with him.

Now Heber the Kenite had moved away from the Kenites, the sons of Hobab, Moses's father-in-law, and pitched his tent beside the oak tree of Zaanannim, which was near Kedesh.

It was reported to Sisera that Barak son of Abinoam had gone up Mount Tabor. Sisera summoned all his nine hundred iron chariots and all the troops who were with him from Harosheth of the Nations to the Wadi Kishon. Then Deborah said to Barak, "Go! This is the day the LORD has handed Sisera over to you. Hasn't the LORD gone before you?" So Barak came down from Mount Tabor with ten thousand men following him.

The LORD threw Sisera, all his charioteers, and all his army into a panic before Barak's assault. Sisera left his chariot and fled on foot. Barak pursued the chariots and the army as far as Harosheth of the Nations, and the whole army of Sisera fell by the sword; not a single man was left. (CSB)

GOD, *thank You for calling and equipping me to lead where You've placed me and for going before me in every battle I must fight. Give me wisdom to know who to lock arms with and how I can lead with strength and discernment. Amen.*

REFLECT

What does this passage teach you about how God views our ability to lead others?

What is God telling you about your leadership potential?

Empowered to Embrace Our Gifts

Then the LORD said to Moses, "Look, I have specifically chosen Bezalel son of Uri, grandson of Hur, of the tribe of Judah. I have filled him with the Spirit of God, giving him great wisdom, ability, and expertise in all kinds of crafts. He is a master craftsman, expert in working with gold, silver, and bronze. He is skilled in engraving and mounting gemstones and in carving wood. He is a master at every craft!"

Exodus 31:1-5 NLT

"I feel like God is calling me to write," I explain sheepishly. The rest of the pastoral staff look at me, puzzled. I had just announced that after seven years of being part of this ministry, I'd be moving back home to be near family and to follow the new path I could no longer deny God was leading me on.

I felt awkward saying those words aloud because I had nothing to show for it. Aside from a few blog posts I'd written, I was calling something into being that I wasn't even sure about. So I could understand why my colleagues were so puzzled. Some of them had known me for over a decade. They had watched me grow from an enthusiastic college student who had a passion for overseas missions and wanted to marry a pastor into a new stay-at-home mom who *became* the pastor.

I had always been so sure of my calling to be in church ministry. I was a missionary/pastor's kid who had served in leadership positions since I was nine, with every skill and gift pointing to a life in ministry.

It was what others saw in me and what I saw in myself, and I had no intention or desire to leave it. But it had become clear to me that God was closing that door in order to open a new one that led to mystery and wonder, doubt and a lot of puzzled looks.

I add, "Like on the internet, a blog maybe . . ." My voice trails off, unsure of where it's headed. And though they—and even I—don't understand what it all means, we nod together in silence. I want to hide in a hole and forget that I even heard God to begin with.

I second-guess this new calling. I wonder why and ask God again, "Are You sure?" Like Gideon, who questioned and pleaded with God for signs over and over, I beg Him to make it clear.

How could I be called to lead with my words? Throughout my education, my writing was always mediocre at best, and I despised academic essays. I was a hands-on, practical-application type of person, not a philosopher or a scholar. Who was I to think that my thoughts mattered or that I even had the skills to write them?

I position these facts before the Lord, making a case for why He's got the wrong person. I tell Him I'll be making a fool of myself—and maybe Him too—if I go down this path. I point out how there are already plenty of talented, well-known people doing the same work, so what good would I be?

He listens to my argument—patient and willing to show me again that He means what He says, that He can give new gifts, new skills, new dreams. In my Bible reading, the story of Bezalel in Exodus 31:1–5 catches my attention. God fills him with His Spirit and gives him great wisdom, ability, and expertise in *all* kinds of crafts. He is anointed to become an artist and entrusted to create beauty in the tabernacle, the dwelling place of God.

That's when I realize I'm not actually thinking little of myself but little of God. If He created the world by speaking it into being, how different was that from what He was doing in my life? God's creative word is powerful, and filling us with His Spirit is a guarantee that He will carry out what He says He will do. Our gifts, like those of Bezalel, are meant to highlight God's genius and bring others into His presence. So embracing our gifts, whether newly discovered or slowly uncovered, is not arrogance but humbly trusting that God knows what He's doing.

Even if it starts with the smallest inkling, even if you and others can't make sense of it, God's calling on your life isn't silly or meant for someone else. He wants to make Himself known uniquely through you.

GOD, *in my limited logic, I often make too little of You. Forgive me for putting You in a box and for dismissing Your word to me when I feel unqualified. You are mysterious, and that isn't something to be afraid of. Thank You that I can trust You and that You entrust me with gifts that will help others experience You. Amen.*

REFLECT

What are some gifts you're uncovering or discovering in this season of your life?

What are some barriers to your fully embracing the gifts God has given you?

Empowered to Feel All Our Feelings

There is an occasion for everything,
and a time for every activity under heaven:
a time to give birth and a time to die;
a time to plant and a time to uproot;
a time to kill and a time to heal;
a time to tear down and a time to build;
a time to weep and a time to laugh;
a time to mourn and a time to dance.

Ecclesiastes 3:1–4 CSB

Recently, I watched the movie *Inside Out* with my family for a movie night. I had popcorn in hand, blankets cozied up, and tissues at the ready because this movie hits me right in the feels. Have you seen it? It's a darling animated film about emotions and feelings, and it's so full of beauty and insight and nostalgia that I just sit with tears in my eyes through the whole thing.

Inside Out tells the story of a girl named Riley, and it does so from the perspective of the feelings that are at the helm of her emotions and therefore her experiences and memories. The feelings manage Riley's dreams, help her develop the islands of personality that make up who she is, and file away her core memories. We meet all of the feelings as they run the giant navigation board somewhere inside Riley's self, but the two main characters are Joy and Sadness.

Joy drives the boat most of the time. She wants Riley to be happy at all costs, believing that joy and cheerfulness are the best—the only—way to feel. She's made sure that all of Riley's core memories are happy ones, and we see Joy exude a fierce love for Riley even in bleak situations.

And then there's Sadness. She's my personal favorite. She's not allowed to touch the board or the memories, because when she does, they turn blue—tinged with sadness. At one point, Joy draws a circle on the floor and tells Sadness to stay in the circle, believing Riley is better off without any blue in her system. But as we watch the story unfold, we learn that Joy and Sadness *must* coexist. Not only is there space for them both, but they *need* each other for the full picture.

Together, Joy and Sadness tell the whole story.

Often, we want to bypass sadness (or any non-happy emotion for that matter) and just get to the good stuff. We tell our kids to stop crying. We tell ourselves not to cry over spilled milk, meaning that some things aren't important enough to be sad about. We don't take our time grieving but rush through the steps to get to the joy we're sure is on the other side.

Spoiler alert: there is no other side.

Grief, sadness, and tears are all part of our stories. We need those benchmark moments when we allow feelings to wash over us, consume us, bring us to our knees. It's when we avoid those feelings that problems arise. When we stuff down the negative feelings, we pay a price.

When we stop the tears, we stop the healing.

It's why I am so grateful that John records how Jesus wept when His friend Lazarus died (John 11:35). I'm grateful we're shown that like us, He grieved the loss of loved ones. I'm grateful that we get to see Jesus being tempted in the wilderness, where He surely experienced a myriad of conflicting emotions. I am so thankful that Jesus took upon Himself the human experience of sadness, because it makes space for my own.

Unlike the character Joy from *Inside Out*, I'm not an optimist by nature. I'm for sure more of a melancholy kind of person, prone to sadness. Often, I feel like I need to push past that and get back to the good stuff—the joy, the dancing. But because of the perfect way Jesus grieved and experienced sadness, I know I also need to feel all of my emotions.

Thanks to the way Jesus lived, fully human and fully divine, there's space for joy and sadness. We are designed to encompass both.

Our memories can be tinged with blue, but we are still whole. We can feel our feelings fiercely, wipe our noses after a good long cry, and still be surprised by times of joy.

There's space and time for it all, and we can live that truth from the inside out.

HEAVENLY FATHER, *thank You for sending Your Son to dwell among us as a man who had friends, family, and feelings. Thank You for the Scriptures, for the stories and experiences that give us glimpses into Jesus's heart— and Yours. Help me to lean deeply into You as I walk through both joy and sadness. Amen.*

REFLECT

Is it easier for you to lean more deeply into joy or sadness?

What can you learn from the way Jesus experienced His emotions?

The Power of Grieving

John 11:17–45

On his arrival, Jesus found that Lazarus had already been in the tomb for four days. Now Bethany was less than two miles from Jerusalem, and many Jews had come to Martha and Mary to comfort them in the loss of their brother. When Martha heard that Jesus was coming, she went out to meet him, but Mary stayed at home.

"Lord," Martha said to Jesus, "if you had been here, my brother would not have died. But I know that even now God will give you whatever you ask."

Jesus said to her, "Your brother will rise again."

Martha answered, "I know he will rise again in the resurrection at the last day."

Jesus said to her, "I am the resurrection and the life. The one who believes in me will live, even though they die; and whoever lives by believing in me will never die. Do you believe this?"

"Yes, Lord," she replied, "I believe that you are the Messiah, the Son of God, who is to come into the world."

After she had said this, she went back and called her sister Mary aside. "The Teacher is here," she said, "and is asking for you." When Mary heard this, she got up quickly and went to him. Now Jesus had not yet entered the village, but was still at the place where Martha had met him. When the Jews who had been with Mary in the house, comforting her, noticed how quickly she got up and went out, they followed her, supposing she was going to the tomb to mourn there.

When Mary reached the place where Jesus was and saw him, she fell at his feet and said, "Lord, if you had been here, my brother would not have died."

When Jesus saw her weeping, and the Jews who had come along with her also weeping, he was deeply moved in spirit and troubled. "Where have you laid him?" he asked.

"Come and see, Lord," they replied.

Jesus wept.

Then the Jews said, "See how he loved him!"

But some of them said, "Could not he who opened the eyes of the blind man have kept this man from dying?"

Jesus, once more deeply moved, came to the tomb. It was a cave with a stone laid across the entrance. "Take away the stone," he said.

"But, Lord," said Martha, the sister of the dead man, "by this time there is a bad odor, for he has been there four days."

Then Jesus said, "Did I not tell you that if you believe, you will see the glory of God?"

So they took away the stone. Then Jesus looked up and said, "Father, I thank you that you have heard me. I knew that you always hear me, but I said this for the benefit of the people standing here, that they may believe that you sent me."

When he had said this, Jesus called in a loud voice, "Lazarus, come out!" The dead man came out, his hands and feet wrapped with strips of linen, and a cloth around his face.

Jesus said to them, "Take off the grave clothes and let him go."

Therefore many of the Jews who had come to visit Mary, and had seen what Jesus did, believed in him.

GOD, *thank You for creating us to be emotional beings. Thank You for welcoming and holding all my feelings—all my grief, pain, anger, and joy. Thank You that I don't have to hide or suppress my emotions from You. Show me how to love others well and to believe in Your power. Amen.*

REFLECT

What can you learn through this passage about God's view of showing emotions and the power of grieving together in community?

What is God saying to you about the power of your emotions and how you express them?

Empowered to Rest

Then Jesus said, "Come to me, all of you who are weary and carry heavy burdens, and I will give you rest. Take my yoke upon you. Let me teach you, because I am humble and gentle at heart, and you will find rest for your souls. For my yoke is easy to bear, and the burden I give you is light."

Matthew 11:28–30 NLT

My throat starts to tickle, but I blame it on allergies I don't have. I have so much work I need to do, and I've been waiting till the house was quiet to get the bulk of it done. I boil some water to make myself some lemon and ginger tea, and I grab a sweater. It's eighty degrees out even at night, and yet my bones feel cold. My joints begin to ache. *I'm not sick. I can't be,* I tell myself.

I find a straggling cough drop in my purse and pop it into my mouth, hoping the menthol will take away the tickle, then make a list of my to-dos. With the professionalism of a procrastinator, I choose the least important thing to start with. I write emails and respond to voice messages. I remember that we don't have carrots for tomorrow's dinner, so I open the Notes app on my phone and jot down what else we need for the week. And because my phone is open, I check Instagram and get sucked into the vortex of scrolling. It's the classic "If you give a mouse a cookie" story where one thing leads to another but never what you first intended to do.

By the time I get to the real work—the hard work—I've crossed off several things (and added some more to the list just so I can cross them off), but the cough drop didn't help. My throat feels scratchy. I try to clear my throat but cough instead. And even though I'm trying to think about work, my head bobs up and down with sleep.

I finally surrender when it feels like my shoulders have frozen over. I drag extra blankets to my room and crawl into bed, burying myself in layers of cotton and fuzziness. I shiver in an effort to get warm and finally concede—I'm sick.

I so often push back against the invitation to rest because I don't feel like I need it. More than that, I don't feel like I *deserve* it. If I haven't pushed myself hard enough, to the limits of my physical strength and mental capacity, rest feels like a luxury I haven't earned. In a society that equates my worth to what and how much I produce, rest is considered optional—an extracurricular activity when or if I have time.

But when I swat away God's invitation to rest, my body can only go for so long. Eventually, it breaks down, and I am forced to slow down, drink more water, take naps, accept my limitations, and trust God's provision. I'm human, and God included rest as part of my design. Therefore, I am empowered to choose rest, create margins in my life and schedule, and go against a culture of burnout.

I'm humbled by my body's reminder that I am not a machine. I am flesh and blood, with life breathed into me every day by our Creator God. I don't need to prove my strength or faithfulness to Him by coming to the end of myself for the sake of others. It's neither holy nor helpful.

Instead, God invites me to come and find rest for my soul because He understands that's exactly what I need. So, I sleep—tired, sick, and beloved.

GENTLE GOD, *I'm so tired. I want to get out of the cycle of busyness and finding my worth in what I produce, but it feels counterintuitive. Teach me to create rhythms that honor the way You designed me, and change the way I think so that I see rest as a must instead of a maybe. Empower me, I pray. Amen.*

REFLECT

How can you incorporate rhythms of rest in your daily, weekly, and monthly schedules?

What is one practice of rest that you'd like to start? For example, take a day off from any sort of producing, walk with a friend, take Sunday naps, or incorporate pauses into your schedule to do deep-breathing exercises.

Empowered to Be Expectant

> Every time I think of you, I give thanks to my God. Whenever I pray, I make my requests for all of you with joy, for you have been my partners in spreading the Good News about Christ from the time you first heard it until now. And I am certain that God, who began the good work within you, will continue his work until it is finally finished on the day when Christ Jesus returns.
>
> Philippians 1:3–6 NLT

When I turned thirty-three, I felt unsettled. At first, I wasn't sure why that age held any significance for me. Eventually, though, I realized: Jesus was thirty-three when He died. And in those thirty-three years, He literally saved the world. What had I done in the same amount of time?

This line of thought sounds ridiculous nearly a decade later, but in the moment it truly caused me some anxiety. Of course, I wasn't actually comparing myself to Jesus. I knew that nobody—including Jesus—expected me to accomplish the same things He did. And I understood that God has a unique plan for each one of us, and His plan for me likely did not follow the same timeline or trajectory as for the Son of God.

And yet, I was a little afraid that my window was closing, that my time for doing anything that mattered was ending, that I'd missed my chance to do whatever it was that God had planned for me. At the age of thirty-three, I feared my life was over.

Again, I am aware of how foolish that sounds. But that kind of perfectionist, defeatist thinking has plagued me for much of my life. Goals, resolutions, bucket lists—these all have crushed my confidence in God's sovereignty over my life. Holding up my life's work to any milestone has always left me overwhelmed with shame and disappointment that I didn't do enough and fear that I never would. If I haven't done it by now—whatever *it* is—then I guess I never will.

This same fear has also crept in every time I've significantly messed up. When I've fallen short—whether intentionally or not—and come face-to-face with the gap between my Lord and my life, I've felt certain that this was the time I went too far. I believed that I'd landed myself too far outside God's will and His plans to find my way back. While I knew that nothing—not even my own bad choices or difficult circumstances—can separate me from the love of God (Rom. 8:39), I began fearing I was too far gone for redemption. Essentially, just like every time I reached a milestone birthday, I presumed my life was over.

Thankfully, God reminds me time and time again that this is not true. Not one word of it! He shines His light on those lies and then points me right back to His promises. He reminds me that as long as I'm living, He's working. He turns my eyes to Scripture and tells me once again that He will continue the good work He began in my life until it is finished.

Not until I turn a certain age.

Not until I mess things up too badly.

Not until someone else derails His plans or mine.

Not until I get sick or busy or distracted or even old.

No! He promises me—and you—that He will finish the good work He started. So rather than feeling doom and gloom, certain that we missed our chance, we can face this day and all the days to come with hope. We can look at how the Lord is working in our lives and feel expectant and excited to see what He's going to do next.

Are you afraid you've missed your chance? That the life God intended for you has passed you by? Do you presume that, after waiting this long, those promises about His plan for you must not be true?

Remember that God never gives up on us. Remember that He has a plan for your life, and until that plan is fulfilled, you can look forward and eagerly expect Him to keep His promises.

LORD, *thank You for giving me hope instead of deadlines. Thank You for continuing to work out Your plans and promises in my life no matter how much I mess up or how many days pass. Please give me a sense of expectant hope for what comes next. I love You, Lord. Amen.*

REFLECT

Think about a time when you feared that you had missed your chance. What has happened since then?

Where do you need to expect God's continued work in your life today?

The Power of Sisterhood

Ruth 1:1–22; 4:13–17

In the days when the judges ruled, there was a famine in the land. So a man from Bethlehem in Judah, together with his wife and two sons, went to live for a while in the country of Moab. The man's name was Elimelek, his wife's name was Naomi, and the names of his two sons were Mahlon and Kilion. They were Ephrathites from Bethlehem, Judah. And they went to Moab and lived there.

Now Elimelek, Naomi's husband, died, and she was left with her two sons. They married Moabite women, one named Orpah and the other Ruth. After they had lived there about ten years, both Mahlon and Kilion also died, and Naomi was left without her two sons and her husband.

When Naomi heard in Moab that the LORD had come to the aid of his people by providing food for them, she and her daughters-in-law prepared to return home from there. With her two daughters-in-law she left the place where she had been living and set out on the road that would take them back to the land of Judah.

Then Naomi said to her two daughters-in-law, "Go back, each of you, to your mother's home. May the LORD show you kindness, as you have shown kindness to your dead husbands and to me. May the LORD grant that each of you will find rest in the home of another husband."

Then she kissed them goodbye and they wept aloud and said to her, "We will go back with you to your people."

But Naomi said, "Return home, my daughters. Why would you come with me? Am I going to have any more sons, who could become your husbands? Return home, my daughters; I am too old to have another husband. Even if I thought there was still hope for me—even if I had a husband tonight and then gave birth to sons—would you wait until they grew up? Would you remain unmarried for them? No, my daughters. It is more bitter for me than for you, because the LORD's hand has turned against me!"

At this they wept aloud again. Then Orpah kissed her mother-in-law goodbye, but Ruth clung to her.

"Look," said Naomi, "your sister-in-law is going back to her people and her gods. Go back with her."

But Ruth replied, "Don't urge me to leave you or to turn back from you. Where you go I will go, and where you stay I will stay. Your people will be my people and your God my God. Where you die I will die, and there I will be buried. May the LORD deal with me, be it ever so severely, if even death separates you and me." When Naomi realized that Ruth was determined to go with her, she stopped urging her.

So the two women went on until they came to Bethlehem. When they arrived in Bethlehem, the whole town was stirred because of them, and the women exclaimed, "Can this be Naomi?"

"Don't call me Naomi," she told them. "Call me Mara, because the Almighty has made my life very bitter. I went away full, but the LORD has brought me back empty. Why call me Naomi? The LORD has afflicted me; the Almighty has brought misfortune upon me."

So Naomi returned from Moab accompanied by Ruth the Moabite, her daughter-in-law, arriving in Bethlehem as the barley harvest was beginning.

So Boaz took Ruth and she became his wife. When he made love to her, the LORD enabled her to conceive, and she gave birth to a son. The women said to Naomi: "Praise be to the LORD, who this day has not left you without a guardian-redeemer. May he become famous throughout Israel! He will renew your life and sustain you in your old age. For your daughter-in-law, who loves you and who is better to you than seven sons, has given him birth."

Then Naomi took the child in her arms and cared for him. The women living there said, "Naomi has a son!" And they named him Obed. He was the father of Jesse, the father of David.

GOD, *thank You for the friends You've given me who are like sisters. Show me how to be steadfast and faithful for the long haul even through difficult times. Amen.*

REFLECT

What does this passage teach you about how God designed us to be in relationship with others for the long haul?

What is God saying to you about your friendships?

Empowered to Be Communal

> But Ruth replied, "Don't ask me to leave you and turn back. Wherever you go, I will go; wherever you live, I will live. Your people will be my people, and your God will be my God. Wherever you die, I will die, and there I will be buried. May the LORD punish me severely if I allow anything but death to separate us!" When Naomi saw that Ruth was determined to go with her, she said nothing more.
>
> Ruth 1:16–18 NLT

My kids peek over my shoulders and see that I'm FaceTiming with my friend Melissa. They shove each other aside trying to get into the camera frame to be the first to say hello.

They wave to her. "Hi, Melissa Eemo!" They chat for a quick second about what they're doing and how their day is going before it's back to play for them and back to the conversation for us.

They call all of my friends *eemo*, which is the Korean word for maternal aunt. It's used to indicate intimacy and respect for our elders, even if we're not blood related. Over the years, my kids have learned to add *eemo* after my friends' names, and it's fostered a closer relationship among us all. Family has come to mean not just our immediate family but a wider circle of friends as well.

The beauty of it has been that my kids become witnesses, prayer partners, and cheerleaders for my friends right alongside me. They've tagged along with me on coffee dates whether or not my friends have kids. They've watched my friends speak at conferences. They've seen my friends' names on book covers at our local Barnes & Noble. They've had access to my community, and this sisterhood I have sets the stage for my kids to learn how to be part of a community too—how to give and receive, how to show up and stand up for each other, how to love well and see God move in each other's lives.

And it goes both ways. My friends have watched my kids grow up from the time I got pregnant. They have witnessed tantrums, but they've also seen more of God through my kids' silliness and childlikeness, their generosity and abounding love.

I think about this give-and-take across generations, about how much we need each other to thrive in our faith, and I'm reminded of the story of Naomi and Ruth.

Because of a famine in her homeland, Naomi and her family move from Bethlehem to the land of Moab. Unfortunately, she loses her husband and ten years later her two sons die, and Naomi is left alone in a foreign land. As a widow with no sons, she has no future to look forward to and no one to care for her, so she decides to return to her homeland and tells her daughters-in-law to go back to their mothers' homes. In tears, Orpah leaves, but Ruth clings tightly to Naomi and insists on staying with her.

When they arrive in Bethlehem, the women of the town ask, "Is it really Naomi?" She responds, "Don't call me Naomi. Instead, call me Mara, for the Almighty has made life very bitter for me" (Ruth 1:20 NLT).

How could Naomi not be bitter about the hand she was dealt? I imagine her relationship with God was bruised, if not broken, from the compounding losses she had suffered. How barren and hopeless she must have felt! And yet, chapter 1 of Ruth closes with this detail: "They arrived in Bethlehem in late spring, at the beginning of the barley harvest" (1:22 NLT).

The barley harvest is where Ruth meets Boaz, a kind and generous man who eventually marries Ruth and takes on the responsibility of caring for her and Naomi. Though Naomi had been bitter, through

Boaz's provision for them she is able to see God's almighty hand working *for* her instead of against her.

With each scoop of barley given by Boaz, with the turn of events that leads to Boaz marrying Ruth, with the love of her daughter-in-law and the birth of Ruth and Boaz's son, Naomi experiences God anew.

Naomi thought she'd have to go it alone after she lost her husband and sons, but Ruth becomes her sister, her community, the one God works through to show Naomi that He is still Almighty God who turns sorrow into joy.

We are not meant to live this life as lone rangers. Our lives are intertwined *so* we can lean on each other and experience God in ways we couldn't have on our own. Naomi and Ruth had each other. My kids and their eemos have each other. Perhaps the invitation for you today is to relinquish your self-sufficiency for the beauty and necessity of sisterhood, of community. God is among us even as He is with each of us.

LORD, *thank You for showing up through my community, my friends. When I can't see or hear You, You still speak through them. Remind me that I need others when I fool myself into thinking that I can do everything by myself. Amen.*

REFLECT

How is God showing Himself to you through your friendships or your community?

How can you show up for someone else?

Empowered to Trust God

When you pass through the waters,
I will be with you,
and the rivers will not overwhelm you.
When you walk through the fire,
you will not be scorched,
and the flame will not burn you.

Isaiah 43:2 CSB

My youngest daughter is fearless. Well, not technically, because thunderstorms still send her running to my bedroom at night. But when it comes to leaping from the couch to the ottoman or hanging off the outside edge of the stairs, she doesn't give a second thought to caution or safety.

It's the same at the swimming pool. This past summer she had nearly outgrown her life jacket. But as a mom who's far from fearless, I insisted she wear it anyway. Even though the arm floaties were a smidge tight. Even though she vowed she was *just fine* without them!

I simply did not trust her swimming skills yet. I did, however, trust that life jacket. That didn't mean I left her alone at the pool. I didn't camp out in a lounge chair, eyes glued to a book or my phone. No, I stayed in the pool with her or nearby while watching closely. But in the split second between seeing her jumping off the side and seeing her head pop back above the surface of the water, I could breathe.

On the rare occasion I let her take off her life jacket, it was a different story. Not only did I have to be in the water, I had to be within an arm's reach. And I absolutely did not breathe from the moment she became airborne until I had her back in my arms above water.

I don't want to oversimplify matters of faith, but for me, trusting God is like putting everyone and everything I care about in a giant life jacket.

Right now, I have a sticky note on my planner with a list of names written on it. It's my urgent prayer list: a friend with breast cancer, two friends going through divorce, a friend whose husband has cancer, a friend whose husband lost his job, a family friend recovering from pneumonia. I haven't written my husband, daughters, or brother on the list, because they never leave my prayers, but at times their needs are no less urgent than these.

If I let myself, I could become completely consumed with fear over each one of those situations. The what-ifs and worst-case scenarios whirl around my brain like a tornado, leaving behind as much damage as an actual twister. Chest pain, shortness of breath, tense muscles, and a flood of tears show up any time my loved ones cross my mind. As I desperately rack my brain for tangible ways to help or clever solutions to suggest, my shoulders reach my ears and my eyes widen to the point of causing a headache. I become completely unhelpful and even discouraging to those I so deeply wish to help and encourage.

Thankfully, I'm not alone in my fear. Though God allows me to go there if I choose, He doesn't leave me in that dark place. He whispers, "Come to me," and offers to take my burden (Matt. 11:28–30). And He reminds me that, just as He vows to be with me when I go through deep waters and raging fires, He's made the same promise to each one of those people on my Post-it prayer list.

God's promises—to love us, to care for us, to be with us no matter what—don't just mean I can trust Him with my own safety and well-being, with my own life and heart and soul. No, He's promised each and every one of us—and each and every one of the people I love—the same things. And while those promises don't necessarily mean we will experience physical healing or safety, they do mean I can trust Him with the hearts and souls of my loved ones as well as with my own.

And what a gift that is! What a relief! Because when we trust God with those we love, not only are we relieved of the anxiety that comes from worrying and attempting to control their lives, but we are actually able to love them better. When we trust God with our loved ones, we don't have to keep them within arm's reach or in a cage or a bubble. We are freed up to love them without pressure. That's when they can see the love of God through us and be encouraged by our trust in Him.

DEAR GOD, *thank You for always being faithful to Your promises. Forgive me for grasping at the illusion of control instead of leaning on You. Remind me of Your faithfulness, and help me trust You more—with my own life and with my loved ones. Amen.*

REFLECT

Think of a loved one you're worried about. What would it look like to love them well by trusting God?

How could trusting God to be your life jacket change things?

The Power of Persistence and Outrageous Hope

1 Samuel 1:1–20

There was a certain man from Ramathaim, a Zuphite from the hill country of Ephraim, whose name was Elkanah son of Jeroham, the son of Elihu, the son of Tohu, the son of Zuph, an Ephraimite. He had two wives; one was called Hannah and the other Peninnah. Peninnah had children, but Hannah had none.

Year after year this man went up from his town to worship and sacrifice to the Lord Almighty at Shiloh, where Hophni and Phinehas, the two sons of Eli, were priests of the Lord. Whenever the day came for Elkanah to sacrifice, he would give portions of the meat to his wife Peninnah and to all her sons and daughters. But to Hannah he gave a double portion because he loved her, and the Lord had closed her womb. Because the Lord had closed Hannah's womb, her rival kept provoking her in order to irritate her. This went on year after year. Whenever Hannah went up to the house of the Lord, her rival provoked her till she wept and would not eat. Her husband Elkanah would say to her, "Hannah, why are you weeping? Why don't you eat? Why are you downhearted? Don't I mean more to you than ten sons?"

Once when they had finished eating and drinking in Shiloh, Hannah stood up. Now Eli the priest was sitting on his chair by the doorpost of the Lord's house. In her deep anguish Hannah prayed to the Lord, weeping bitterly. And she made a vow, saying, "Lord Almighty, if you will only look on your servant's misery and remember me, and not forget your servant but give her a son, then I will give him to the Lord for all the days of his life, and no razor will ever be used on his head."

As she kept on praying to the Lord, Eli observed her mouth. Hannah was praying in her heart, and her lips were moving but her voice was not heard. Eli thought she was drunk and said to her, "How long are you going to stay drunk? Put away your wine."

"Not so, my lord," Hannah replied, "I am a woman who is deeply troubled. I have not been drinking wine or beer; I was pouring out my soul to the Lord. Do not take your servant for a wicked woman; I have been praying here out of my great anguish and grief."

Eli answered, "Go in peace, and may the God of Israel grant you what you have asked of him."

She said, "May your servant find favor in your eyes." Then she went her way and ate something, and her face was no longer downcast.

Early the next morning they arose and worshiped before the Lord and then went back to their home at Ramah. Elkanah made love to his wife Hannah, and the Lord remembered her. So in the course of time Hannah became pregnant and gave birth to a son. She named him Samuel, saying, "Because I asked the Lord for him."

GOD, *thank You for hearing my every prayer, my every cry. Thank You for not tiring of listening to and answering me because You love me. Give me the stamina to press on with hope and faith while I wait. Amen.*

REFLECT

What can we learn from this passage about how God feels about our persistent prayers and outrageous hope, even in the face of repeated disappointment?

What do you need in order to keep hoping and trusting God for the thing you're waiting for?

Empowered to Be Hospitable

Don't forget to show hospitality to strangers, for some who have
done this have entertained angels without realizing it!

Hebrews 13:2 NLT

I'll never forget 2020 for many obvious reasons—politics, a global
pandemic, and schooling my kids at home, just to name a few. But
one of the best things I'll remember is how in the middle of that global
pandemic, I was on the receiving end of incredible hospitality without
leaving home or inviting anyone into my home.

That autumn, I had my fourth child. There are five years between
him and his next oldest sibling, so it had been a while since we'd had
a baby. Plus, this time I was pregnant during a pandemic, which was
a strange and lonely experience. I went by myself to every doctor
appointment and ultrasound. My husband would drop me off at the
curb of the clinic but was not allowed to accompany me inside due
to COVID restrictions. While I was in labor, every doctor, nurse, and
staff member who entered my room wore a mask and full-body PPE
so that only their eyes were visible. No visitors were allowed after
the baby arrived, neither in our hospital room nor in our home. No
family waited to welcome us home from the hospital. There was no
family brunch after our baby's (socially distanced, masked, outdoor)
baptism. There were no playdates with friends. No one outside of our
household held him for months.

The last pregnancy and birth I would ever experience was so lonely, so scary, and so raw with fear of the unknown and feeling out of control. It was overwhelming.

Until the people in my village got down to business to care for our family.

My coworkers at (in)courage arranged a surprise online baby shower. They invited all of our writers to log into a video call that I thought was just our regular team meeting. They even coordinated with my husband and sister to receive, hide, and then bring out the gifts they'd all sent—and also to bring me dessert!

My sister threw me an outdoor "sprinkle," a mini baby shower. Complete with my few closest family and friends, who all wore masks and gave only air hugs, there were individually packaged treats, personal serving utensils, and only one game, which we played while sitting in our chairs that were placed at least six feet apart. My best friend, who lives in another state, surprised me by driving the eight hours to attend the party!

After our baby was born, friends from my church committee delivered meals to our doorstep every Tuesday for six weeks. My mom did our laundry, washing our clothes that were covered in baby spit-up and kid dirt. My sister texted me every day for weeks, asking for pictures of the baby because she knew I wasn't getting to show him off enough to the world. (Such a mom thing to think of, right?) Friends and family phoned, emailed, and helped the kids with their schoolwork via video calls, and countless people prayed for us.

I cried with gratitude almost every day. It wasn't about the actual gifts or acts of service, beautiful and needed and wonderful as they were. It was about the hearts behind them.

The hospitality I was shown by my friends and family was a balm. The care and love we received was absolute hospitality, the likes of which I'd never experienced before. And frankly, it changed my view of hospitality.

Defined as "the friendly reception and treatment of guests or strangers,"[1] hospitality often brings to mind images of parties, dinner around a heaping table, or coffee shared at a kitchen counter. It makes me think of holiday gatherings, family getting together to celebrate birthdays, and cheering on our favorite team with friends (and snacks!) during a football game.

Of course, none of this was possible during that season, and yet hospitality is the best description of what I was so generously given. Because my friends were empowered to be hospitable despite the strange circumstances, I was beautifully loved by my community. And because of their hospitality, when I look back I don't remember a time of loneliness and fear. I remember a time of friendship, home, and love.

When we love others well, we're empowered to share hospitality in any way we can, blessing both the giver and the recipient.

LORD, *may I give—and receive—generous hospitality. Urge me to go out of my way to bless others, and help me to both offer and accept hospitality in all its forms. Give me eyes to see who needs it, and provide me with the means to be hospitable. Amen.*

REFLECT

What is one way you have recently received hospitality?

How can you offer hospitality to another?

1. Dictionary.com, s.v. "hospitality," accessed April 15, 2021, https://www.dictionary.com/browse/hospitality.

Empowered to Be Angry

Jesus entered the Temple and began to drive out all the people buying and selling animals for sacrifice. He knocked over the tables of the money changers and the chairs of those selling doves. He said to them, "The Scriptures declare, 'My Temple will be called a house of prayer,' but you have turned it into a den of thieves!"

Matthew 21:12–13 NLT

I end the call, stunned, unable to comprehend what just happened. The conversation was not what I had anticipated. I thought—and perhaps naively hoped—the call was about a potential writing opportunity, but instead I was being accused of plagiarism. Her allegations were cushioned with niceness and a chipper tone, but nonetheless, she had shredded my integrity with no grounded basis.

I sit frozen, phone in hand, replaying the conversation over and over again in my head. *Surely, she couldn't have meant it,* I reason. I turn the words this way and that to see it from every vantage point, to give her the benefit of the doubt. But still, her intent pierces through, accusing me of wrongdoing and threatening to silence me.

Confusion clarifies into anger, and my entire body throbs. How many times have I been silenced for the comfort of another? How many times have I been made small so another could take up more space—the space that was intended for me as a woman and especially an Asian American woman?

Shaking, I text my mentor, who immediately understands the situation. She's seen this happen to other women of color, and she instructs me to email the woman and call out her actions for what they are—blatant intimidation, racist assumptions, and character defamation.

Sadness and anger swirl together inside me. I lament that I'm one of many, *many* women of color who are regularly silenced, pushed aside, and relegated to overgeneralized stereotypes of who we're supposed to be.

I open my laptop to write the email, but I hesitate. I wonder if I'm being like Jesus or if my anger disqualifies me. Is this a time to turn the other cheek? To stay silent as He did when He was spat on? Or is this a time to flip tables because the current system marginalizes some people and keeps them out? To speak truth to those in power so they can see the harm they cause even with all their good intentions?

I place my fingers on the keys and type each word deliberately. I sign the email with my full name as a way to stand tall, even if it's only in black letters on a screen. I choose not to be timid or quiet as I had been raised to believe a woman should be. I will not be made small by someone who thinks having power by position gives her the right to lord it over me.

I hit send and collapse on the couch, vulnerable and weak. The heightened energy of anger subsides as the tears flow, and I hug a pillow tight against my chest as if it will soothe my aching heart.

Anger is good and needed when wrong is done to us or to anyone else. It is an appropriate response when we experience or witness injustice, abuse, or even the smallest belittling of the image of God in us. It will often guide us toward action, whether it means marching in the streets to protest or crying out in prayer till our voices are hoarse. It can move us to speak up for the first time, set boundaries with a firm no, or call out socially accepted norms that perpetuate harmful thinking.

Sometimes anger may look like grief. Before He entered the temple, Jesus rode into Jerusalem on a donkey, and when He saw the city and its people, He wept (Luke 19:41–44). He lamented. He longed for things to be made right, and He understood the cost He would have to bear to bring redemption.

Other times, anger will look like flipping tables because the evils of greed and power have become so seamlessly twisted with religion that the only way to bring attention to the injustice is to cause a ruckus.

Our faith in Jesus doesn't cancel out anger. Instead, being like Him means becoming angry at the right things so that things will be made right.

GOD OF JUSTICE, *thank You for showing me that I can be angry, even that I must be angry when I see wrong being done and perpetuated. If timidity and silence have been my burden to bear, break me from that yoke and free me. Give me courage when I'm afraid to stand tall and speak out because I've become so used to being small. Help me to harness my anger into action that brings freedom to others as well. Amen.*

REFLECT

What injustice has caused you to be angry recently?

How does Jesus's example of becoming angry guide you to harness your anger to promote acts of justice?

Emotional

The Power of Righteous Anger

Psalm 109:1–5, 21–31

My God, whom I praise,
  do not remain silent,
for people who are wicked and deceitful
  have opened their mouths against me;
  they have spoken against me with lying tongues.
With words of hatred they surround me;
  they attack me without cause.
In return for my friendship they accuse me,
  but I am a man of prayer.
They repay me evil for good,
  and hatred for my friendship.

. . . .

But you, Sovereign LORD,
  help me for your name's sake;
  out of the goodness of your love, deliver me.
For I am poor and needy,
  and my heart is wounded within me.
I fade away like an evening shadow;
  I am shaken off like a locust.
My knees give way from fasting;
  my body is thin and gaunt.
I am an object of scorn to my accusers;
  when they see me, they shake their heads.

Help me, LORD my God;
    save me according to your unfailing love.
Let them know that it is your hand,
    that you, LORD, have done it.
While they curse, may you bless;
    may those who attack me be put to shame,
    but may your servant rejoice.
May my accusers be clothed with disgrace
    and wrapped in shame as in a cloak.
With my mouth I will greatly extol the LORD;
    in the great throng of worshipers I will praise him.
For he stands at the right hand of the needy,
    to save their lives from those who would condemn them.

GOD, *thank You that You see the truth of what is happening to me. Thank You that I am not left alone and vulnerable with those who attack me or my character but that You are my defense and refuge. Amen.*

REFLECT

What can you learn from this passage about how God views anger as a response to injustice?

What can you learn about who God is to you when you experience injustice?

Empowered to Be Strong

Do not fear, for I am with you;
do not be afraid, for I am your God.
I will strengthen you; I will help you;
I will hold on to you with my righteous right hand.

Isaiah 41:10 CSB

Like millions of moviegoers, I love superhero stories. In particular, I've enjoyed watching (repeatedly) *Wonder Woman* and *Captain Marvel*. Certainly, it's fun to cheer for these women as they take on villains and emerge victorious, especially when we're used to seeing mostly men in such heroic roles. But what moves me most is the moment when each of these superheroes steps into her power and realizes her role in the supernatural war being fought.

In *Wonder Woman*, we see Diana climb out of the trenches, intent on helping those in need, and then walk through a storm of bullets to allow her team to advance safely behind her. As she plants her feet and holds up her shield for cover, the music swells and she doesn't say a word. We don't know what's going through her mind as bullets rain down on her and she's attacked by what feels like an endless amount of ammunition. We hear the music and watch her take hit after hit, and we see her standing strong the whole time.

In *Captain Marvel*, when Carol Danvers faces down her biggest opponent, it happens within her subconscious. For much of this internal battle, we see her sitting on the floor, restrained and unmoving. Those observing her from the outside have no idea of the war raging in her mind as the enemy tries to thwart her efforts to save entire worlds.

In both stories, these supernaturally strong women are fighting battles that we cannot fully comprehend. In both stories, they are only able to defeat their enemies after ignoring their team's advice to stand down or their enemy's taunting to give up. They are victorious only by unleashing the inner strength and power they had been given.

Now, you and I are not superheroes. Obviously I know that, no matter how many times I've watched those movies. However, I do think we have a lot in common with Wonder Woman and Captain Marvel.

How many times have you fought a battle that nobody else could see? How many times have you been under siege and on the verge of collapsing while standing strong on the outside? How many times have you looked at the challenge in front of you and been told, "You can't do it"? How many times have you taken stock of your situation and told yourself that?

"I can't do this."

How often have I whispered, shouted, cried those words? I've lost count. I'm sure God knows, though, how many times I've realized that I cannot bear the burdens of the world or even just those that affect me personally. I trust that God knows every single time I'm fighting a war, even if nobody else notices.

So many of us are fighting battles that nobody else knows about. Addiction. Abuse. Chronic pain. Crippling debt. Anxiety. Struggles with our kids, our marriages, our friendships, our careers, our churches. We go to war alone, exhausted, and relying solely on our own strength.

No wonder we feel like giving up and shouting, "I can't do this!"

The good news is that while we are never going to become superheroes, we are given supernatural strength by God. He never asks us to be strong enough to fight every battle—or any battle! Instead, He promises to be with us, to help us and protect us, and to give us the strength we need.

No matter what challenge you're facing today, you aren't facing it alone. And you don't have to do it on your own. Ask God to give you strength, and do not be afraid, for He is your God.

HEAVENLY FATHER, *I'm not a superhero, and I need Your help. This thing I'm facing is too much, and I can't handle it on my own. I can't do this. Please give me strength to face the struggle, to fight what I need to fight, and to rely on You through it all. In Jesus's name, amen.*

REFLECT

What battle are you fighting that might be invisible to most people?

How are you asking God to stand with you and give you strength?

Empowered to Live with Purpose

> Now when David had served God's purpose in his own genera-
> tion, he fell asleep; he was buried with his ancestors and his body
> decayed.
>
> Acts 13:36

"You keep missing the train, Auntie Grace!" they giggled. I had been babysitting these girls long enough that they had heard about my many friends who had gotten married, while I had stayed single or dated to no avail. We sprawled across the living room floor, with snacks and books laid out around us like sunrays, and laughed together at my misfortune. It was the perfect analogy for how I felt. As I waved my friends off on the train of matrimonial bliss, I was left behind, standing on the platform of a standstill life.

Growing up, the message I heard from society and the church, from parents and the pulpit, was that marriage and motherhood were the ultimate roles God intended for me as a young woman. Together, they were *the* purpose of my life. The constant barrage of this view led me to believe that I couldn't be whole without my other half and that life—real life—wasn't going to start for me until I got married.

But no sooner had I walked down the aisle to say "I do" than people began telling us it was time to have kids. It seemed that getting on the marriage train wasn't enough. In order to live a full life and reach the pinnacle of womanhood, I needed to start a family. I had a career in church ministry and was pursuing the calling God had for my life. I was leading with my gifts and investing in others. I felt fulfilled by my work and my relationships. But those things were considered secondary. Every week, congregation members would stop me in the hallways or the back of the worship room, grab my hand with genuine concern, and ask me when I was going to have kids.

And just as it had taken longer than expected to find a husband, it took longer than I wanted and a roller coaster of twists and turns to get pregnant.

I entered the world of motherhood ready to experience its wonder and the satisfaction of being all that I was made to be, but instead I lost my bearings. I didn't know who I was anymore or what my purpose was supposed to be. I felt empty instead of fulfilled, disoriented instead of grounded.

I questioned what I had been taught: If this was the primary purpose of womanhood, what did that mean for anyone who wasn't married or didn't have children? What did it mean for me personally, as I seemed to have everything I should want but still found it all lacking? What was living with purpose supposed to look like?

I didn't know whom to turn to for the answers, for guidance, but the words of Acts 13:36 began to repeat themselves in my heart: "Now when David had served God's purpose in his own generation, he fell asleep; he was buried with his ancestors and his body decayed." Years earlier, a mentor of mine had pointed out this passage to me as a reminder that we are all made with and for a purpose.

At that time, I took it to mean that we each have one purpose to accomplish in our lives and that our job is to figure out that sole thing and pursue it with abandon. As a young woman, I was taught that my purpose was motherhood and marriage. But in the early days of parenthood and in the years since then, I've come to understand that our purpose and vision shift according to the seasons we are in. There will never be a time when our life doesn't serve a purpose—even if we feel like it doesn't.

I used to feel like I was perpetually behind my peers, always waving them off on wild adventures while my life stayed the same. The reality was and still is that their life isn't mine, their timeline isn't mine, and God's purpose for their life won't always align with His purpose for mine.

So, we don't have to wait for "one day" to come or for the right person or circumstance to materialize before we can live out our purpose for our generation. As long as we have breath, we can live out God's purpose. Whether it's becoming an expert in your field of work, volunteering in a soup kitchen, surviving another day with chronic pain, playing with your children, writing for an audience of ten or ten thousand—whatever it looks like for you in this season, know that your being faithful to the things God has set in front of you now is what living with purpose really means.

LORD, *I want my life to mean something, but sometimes it's hard to find significance in what I do, especially when it seems too ordinary for Your glory. Remind me that Your glory is all around, woven into every season of my life. Beyond the traditional roles society puts on women, You are working out Your purpose in and through me no matter the relationships I'm in, the positions I hold, or how circumstances change. Amen.*

REFLECT

What "one day" have you been waiting for?

What do you think your purpose is in this season?

The Power of Choosing Jesus over Everything Else

Luke 10:38–42

As Jesus and his disciples were on their way, he came to a village where a woman named Martha opened her home to him. She had a sister called Mary, who sat at the Lord's feet listening to what he said. But Martha was distracted by all the preparations that had to be made. She came to him and asked, "Lord, don't you care that my sister has left me to do the work by myself? Tell her to help me!"

"Martha, Martha," the Lord answered, "you are worried and upset about many things, but few things are needed—or indeed only one. Mary has chosen what is better, and it will not be taken away from her."

GOD, *thank You for the model of Jesus and the life He lived on earth. Please keep me mindful of the way my need for You eclipses any other priority I might have. Amen.*

REFLECT

What does this story teach you about what God sees as most important?

What is God saying to you if you're caught up in placing priority on projects and tasks?

Empowered to Be More Than Conquerors

What, then, are we to say about these things? If God is for us, who is against us? He did not even spare his own Son but gave him up for us all. How will he not also with him grant us everything? Who can bring an accusation against God's elect? God is the one who justifies. Who is the one who condemns? Christ Jesus is the one who died, but even more, has been raised; he also is at the right hand of God and intercedes for us. Who can separate us from the love of Christ? Can affliction or distress or persecution or famine or nakedness or danger or sword? As it is written:

> Because of you
> we are being put to death all day long;
> we are counted as sheep to be slaughtered.

No, in all these things we are more than conquerors through him who loved us. For I am persuaded that neither death nor life, nor angels nor rulers, nor things present nor things to come, nor powers, nor height nor depth, nor any other created thing will be able to separate us from the love of God that is in Christ Jesus our Lord.

Romans 8:31–39 CSB

During my college years, I worked as a counselor at a Bible camp. Each summer I packed up all of my necessary belongings in one gigantic blue plastic tote, loaded the tote and myself into my old red Toyota, and headed north. The camp I worked at was in northern Minnesota, six miles down a dirt road and nestled among pine trees that gave way to an expansive lakeshore. It was a place where the Holy Spirit roamed as free as the campers, filling hearts and opening eyes and giving new life.

We spent our days playing games, studying the Bible, doing arts and crafts, swimming, singing, and laughing. We did so much laughing in that place! I felt closer to the Lord at camp than at any other time or place in my life, and I know I wasn't the only one. There was room for the Lord to move and an expectancy that He would.

But even more meaningful than the memories of fun and laughter, of Scripture study and crafts, is the memory of how we began each day at camp.

Every single morning, each camper and staff member gathered around a flagpole. (There wasn't actually a flag on the pole, but it served as a pretty nice gathering spot.) One staffer was appointed to lead each part of the morning opening, which began with a silly song to wake up our bodies. Next was a prayer in which we asked God to bless our day. And finally, a word of Scripture.

This was not simply a Bible reading. What happened was this: the appointed staffer would pray over and choose what we called a *decree*. A decree was something each of us is because of God, as found in Scripture. We had a full list of these decrees that kept growing throughout the summer, and each morning we would holler one out at the top of our lungs.

I am a child of God!
I am beloved!
I am forgiven!
I am chosen!
I am fearfully and wonderfully made!

Hundreds of kids exclaiming these truths first thing in the morning? It was a powerful and holy way to begin each day.

And when it was my turn to lead, I would almost always choose my personal favorite: *I am more than a conqueror through Christ!*

You don't have to be a camp counselor or a camper (or be anywhere near a camp) to cry out this truth. Whatever the challenge, whatever the battle, the Lord has promised that we can overcome. We are *more* than conquerors—equipped and ready to fight whether we feel up to the challenge or not. That's right. Even if we don't feel ready, God is for us. God loves us. And nothing can separate us from that love.

No matter what. Full stop.

Friend, walk confidently with your head held high into that battle that scares, accuses, or condemns. God has gone first, and nothing can come between you and His love. Because of His great love, you are more than a conqueror.

LORD, *give me the confidence of an early-morning camper. Help me stand on the truth that I am already more than a conqueror, equipped for whatever fight I face. Thank You for Your love, bold and complete. Amen.*

REFLECT

Is it easy or hard for you to believe you are *more* than a conqueror? Why do you think that is?

How can you walk forward boldly with your head held high?

Empowered to Live Fully Alive

I have come that they may have life, and have it to the full.

John 10:10

Over the years my kids have watched a lot of VeggieTales, and therefore so have I. Which is surely the only explanation for why one of the tracks on the playlist of my mind is the voice of a stuffy asparagus saying, "STOP BEING SO SILLY!"

While the voice and the exact words are the result of watching a cartoon with my kids, my tendency to temper any silliness I might feel or exhibit comes from somewhere else. A combination of innate personality, upbringing, and life experience created in me a belief that being serious is better than being silly.

Or at least a belief that being serious is *safer* than being silly.

I remember spending the night at a friend's house for a slumber party. Between giggling about the boys we liked at school and emptying her parents' pantry of every chip and cookie we could find, we danced around her bedroom singing along to the radio. Well, my friends did that. Though I grabbed a hairbrush to use as a pretend microphone, I couldn't bring myself to actually sing. And dance? No way!

As a member of every choir my school and church had to offer, it seems strange that I wasn't willing to sing out loud in front of my friends. But I was paralyzed with fear that I wouldn't sound good enough or that I'd look—you guessed it—silly. And if I looked silly or sang off-key? Well, surely my friends would mock me forever and I would die from embarrassment!

Perfectionism—an intense desire to control every single factor in my life and the paralyzing fear of being seen as less-than—kept me in serious-not-silly mode for years.

Eventually (many VeggieTales videos later), I realized this super-serious, ultra-controlling person wasn't actually who I wanted to be and might not be how God wanted me to live. About fifteen years after sitting stiff and somber at my friend's slumber party while the others relaxed and had a blast singing along to the radio, I'd grown into the so-called mom of every group I ever joined. I always had tissues and bandages in my purse, I followed all the rules (unless you count the speed limit), and one of my most commonly used phrases was, "Well, *someone's* got to do it!"

But then I took a StrengthsFinder personality test. Learning that one of my top strengths is responsibility shook me. I'm not sure what I was expecting from my test results, but that wasn't it. I didn't want to be responsible. I wanted to be fun and passionate and funny and amazing!

Don't worry. I'm fully aware that responsible people can also be all those things. But in the moment, I felt certain I was being painted into a corner where all I was good for was making lists and reminding people to turn in their invoices. Next step? Yelling at "those kids" to get off my lawn!

Somehow I had become confused about so many things. I was confusing serious for boring, responsible for elderly and grouchy, and living for trying to control my life and prevent any pain that might come from being seen as less-than. I confused my God-given tendency of being responsible for a guarantee that taking care of everything and keeping a straight face at all times would keep me safe.

Instead, it just kept me from living.

That evaluation of my strengths doesn't get all the credit for my transformation into a person who lives a little more. Studying God's

Word and seeing how Jesus specifically came to give us abundant life (not safe or controlled or somber life) also opened my eyes and gave me the freedom to lighten up. Remembering that the only one in control is God and the only safety I can ever be guaranteed is salvation through Jesus Christ has helped show me that real, abundant life is so much better than tenuous, temporary control.

If you have a hard time letting go and living abundantly, ask God to relinquish your grip on the things you think will keep you safe. Ask Him to show you how to live fully alive, how to delight in Him and the gifts He gives, and how to share those gifts with others around you.

A few days ago, when I was playing with my youngest daughter, she said, "Mommy! You are *so* silly!" And without missing a beat or hearing a single vegetable in my head, I said, "I know! Isn't it great?"

LORD, *thank You for the gifts of laughter and sunshine and dance parties and roly-poly puppies and all the delights of this world. Thank You for the freedom to live an abundant life, knowing that I don't have to be perfect and that I am loved even if I snort when I laugh. Please keep my heart light and my focus on You. In Jesus's name, amen.*

REFLECT

What would it look like for you to be more fully alive in Christ?

What holds you back from living into the fullness of life that Jesus calls us to?

The Power in Taking Things Personally

Genesis 30:1–24

When Rachel saw that she was not bearing Jacob any children, she became jealous of her sister. So she said to Jacob, "Give me children, or I'll die!"

Jacob became angry with her and said, "Am I in the place of God, who has kept you from having children?"

Then she said, "Here is Bilhah, my servant. Sleep with her so that she can bear children for me and I too can build a family through her."

So she gave him her servant Bilhah as a wife. Jacob slept with her, and she became pregnant and bore him a son. Then Rachel said, "God has vindicated me; he has listened to my plea and given me a son." Because of this she named him Dan.

Rachel's servant Bilhah conceived again and bore Jacob a second son. Then Rachel said, "I have had a great struggle with my sister, and I have won." So she named him Naphtali.

When Leah saw that she had stopped having children, she took her servant Zilpah and gave her to Jacob as a wife. Leah's servant Zilpah bore Jacob a son. Then Leah said, "What good fortune!" So she named him Gad.

Leah's servant Zilpah bore Jacob a second son. Then Leah said, "How happy I am! The women will call me happy." So she named him Asher.

During wheat harvest, Reuben went out into the fields and found some mandrake plants, which he brought to his mother Leah. Rachel said to Leah, "Please give me some of your son's mandrakes."

But she said to her, "Wasn't it enough that you took away my husband? Will you take my son's mandrakes too?"

"Very well," Rachel said, "he can sleep with you tonight in return for your son's mandrakes."

So when Jacob came in from the fields that evening, Leah went out to meet him. "You must sleep with me," she said. "I have hired you with my son's mandrakes." So he slept with her that night.

God listened to Leah, and she became pregnant and bore Jacob a fifth son. Then Leah said, "God has rewarded me for giving my servant to my husband." So she named him Issachar.

Leah conceived again and bore Jacob a sixth son. Then Leah said, "God has presented me with a precious gift. This time my husband will treat me with honor, because I have borne him six sons." So she named him Zebulun.

Some time later she gave birth to a daughter and named her Dinah.

Then God remembered Rachel; he listened to her and enabled her to conceive. She became pregnant and gave birth to a son and said, "God has taken away my disgrace." She named him Joseph, and said, "May the Lord add to me another son."

GOD, *thank You for creating me with a full range of emotions that go so deep, taking things personally is the only way to experience them. Yet, Lord, help minimize any feelings of jealousy, envy, and entitlement before they take root in my heart. Amen.*

REFLECT

What can we learn from this passage about the power of taking things personally?

What is God teaching you about His love from the story of Rachel and Leah?

Empowered to Work

She considers a field and buys it;
> out of her earnings she plants a vineyard.
She sets about her work vigorously;
> her arms are strong for her tasks. . . .

She makes linen garments and sells them,
> and supplies the merchants with sashes.
She is clothed with strength and dignity;
> she can laugh at the days to come.
She speaks with wisdom,
> and faithful instruction is on her tongue.

Proverbs 31:16–17, 24–26

With all the eagerness of an impressionable, young college student, I listened to the poised women on the stage discuss becoming a Proverbs 31 woman. They sat on velvet couches, their dress and demeanor fitting right in with the minimalist decor of the set. They spoke with such ease, such confidence, that I had no doubt they were already the ideal Proverbs 31 women.

I soaked in their wisdom on being a wife of noble character, more precious than rubies, and, of utmost importance, on being a woman who doesn't put stock in her beauty but who fears the Lord. I scribbled messy notes in my journal and went home with the goal of becoming like the women I saw on stage.

Over time, I listened to sermons, did Bible studies, and went to women's retreats about this same topic. It seemed that the exemplary Christian woman was a wife, whose main goal was to serve her husband, her family, and God. She didn't have to be beautiful, but she did have to be put together on the outside in some way—whether in the appearance of her body, her home, or her children. She was most likely a stay-at-home mom whose husband was the main breadwinner. She was often of a comfortable socioeconomic status, able to host and be available to her community. She was generous and kind, and she loved the Lord.

I made it my goal to be this kind of woman. I didn't have all of those qualities, but I was determined to grow into the "right" mold so that I could be exemplary too.

But I was ambitious in other ways as well. I had leadership skills, which placed me in church ministry positions where I led both men and women. I had passions separate from my husband's that I wanted to pursue and that I could use to bless people. I liked to host and create space in my home for others, but I also loved to work outside the home, investing in my community, mentoring young people, and contributing to our finances alongside my husband.

My idea of what a Proverbs 31 woman was supposed to be seemed to clash with how God had made me, and the older I got, the greater the gap widened between the supposed ideal and my reality.

Once I became a mom, it wasn't long before well-meaning women at church began to offer unsolicited advice on how I ought to be, and their shoulds pushed me to take a closer look at Proverbs 31.

What am I missing? Am I not the woman I'm supposed to be? And if not, who does God say I am to be?

As I read through this famous passage again, I realized that the bulk of what I had been taught was only a small portion of what that chapter is really about.

The epilogue of Proverbs 31 is mostly about a woman who is strong and diligent, a provider for her community and family. She is shrewd and generous, a businesswoman who knows what she's doing. She is clothed with dignity and is grounded in strength. She is a wise teacher and is honored for the work she does.

God created us all—women and men—to work, to care for ourselves and this world, and to look after one another (Gen. 1:28), and the Proverbs 31 woman is an example of just that.

As women, we won't all play the same roles, but we are *all* called and empowered to work—whether that's serving our families in the home or becoming bosses and leaders outside the home. We are capable, strong, and noble when we do the work we're called to do.

GOD, *thank You for making me in Your image and for giving me purpose and agency to become all that You made me to be. You created each of us to be different, and I'm grateful that there are many ways we can become women who fear You above all. Help me to work diligently and faithfully and to become more fully who You designed me to be. Amen.*

REFLECT

How has the "ideal" Proverbs 31 woman hindered you from becoming who you were meant to be?

Since we are all empowered to work, what work is God calling you to do?

The Power of Resurrection

Acts 9:36–42

In Joppa there was a disciple named Tabitha (in Greek her name is Dorcas); she was always doing good and helping the poor. About that time she became sick and died, and her body was washed and placed in an upstairs room. Lydda was near Joppa; so when the disciples heard that Peter was in Lydda, they sent two men to him and urged him, "Please come at once!"

Peter went with them, and when he arrived he was taken upstairs to the room. All the widows stood around him, crying and showing him the robes and other clothing that Dorcas had made while she was still with them.

Peter sent them all out of the room; then he got down on his knees and prayed. Turning toward the dead woman, he said, "Tabitha, get up." She opened her eyes, and seeing Peter she sat up. He took her by the hand and helped her to her feet. Then he called for the believers, especially the widows, and presented her to them alive. This became known all over Joppa, and many people believed in the Lord.

GOD, *thank You for the promise of resurrection where I may only see death and for the power I have in me because of Christ's resurrection. Awaken my soul to the truth that You are not done with me yet. Amen.*

REFLECT

What does this story teach you about God's ability and desire to resurrect any dead thing?

What is it that you need God's resurrection power for?

Empowered to Be Loved by God

> The LORD your God is with you,
> the Mighty Warrior who saves.
> He will take great delight in you;
> in his love he will no longer rebuke you,
> but will rejoice over you with singing.
>
> Zephaniah 3:17

I struggle with perfectionism and the desire to be in control. The two go hand in hand, really.

Work projects? I take pride in executing my work perfectly and being known for doing my job well.

Mothering? It's hard for me to resist the notion that my kids are my report card, that their behavior is a reflection of my parenting (instead of what it actually is—*their* behavior).

My home? I never clean as much as I do in the hour before company comes over. I'm like a whirling dervish with a vacuum. It's not a good look for me.

In a twisted way, there's something comforting about being in control, about completing tasks perfectly.

It's embarrassing to admit, but I never really saw my perfectionist and controlling tendencies until I had kids. You know the saying that kids are mirrors? It's true, and not always in a good way. I began to see my worst habits and most unflattering characteristics making appearances in my miniature me's, and I wanted to squash the behavior before it could become rooted in their little hearts because I knew the pain it could—and would—bring. So at the slightest hint of my kids trying to behave their way into my heart, to earn my love, or to control their way into perfection, I give them huge hugs and many words of reassurance that there is *nothing* they can do to earn my love. There is nothing they can *do* to earn my love. There is nothing they can do to *earn* my love. They simply have it. All my love. No matter what. Forever.

And then one day it was like a light bulb went off in my own heart: God says the same thing to us. God's love isn't something we earn by doing, by behaving, by controlling or being perfect.

There is *nothing* we can do to earn God's love.

There is nothing we can *do* to earn God's love.

There is nothing we can do to *earn* God's love.

By God's goodness and grace, He freely offers us His love—no perfect behavior or tally of earnings required. It's one of the best, most incredible gifts we're given—and often the hardest to accept.

The world rewards good behavior, and we're taught from a young age that we need to work hard to earn things, right? God takes all that and turns it upside down.

The verses from Zephaniah illustrate such a beautiful juxtaposition. *Empowered* is an action word, and yet these verses show God as the one taking action, while our role is fairly passive. God is the one saving us. God is the one rejoicing. God is the one singing. God is the one loving us no matter what. There's no way we can perfect our way into His heart or earn His love.

We can feel weaker, more desperate, more rock bottom than we've ever felt before, and we're still loved by God.

His love doesn't depend on us.

I whisper those words to my kids during tantrums, sad moments, and difficult times, reminding them that there is nothing they can do to earn my love; they simply have it forever. I pray we all take in the love we so undeservedly receive.

We are empowered for something we have no power over. And that is the best news ever.

> **LORD**, *I am humbled by Your love. Thank You for such a gift. Empower me to accept it, to remember that I cannot earn my way into Your heart, that I cannot control Your love for me. Give me the confidence to live this out in my everyday life. Amen.*

REFLECT

Is it difficult for you to accept the unearned love of God? Why or why not?

How does it feel to know that God rejoices over you with singing?

The Power of Giving Until It Hurts

Luke 7:36–50

When one of the Pharisees invited Jesus to have dinner with him, he went to the Pharisee's house and reclined at the table. A woman in that town who lived a sinful life learned that Jesus was eating at the Pharisee's house, so she came there with an alabaster jar of perfume. As she stood behind him at his feet weeping, she began to wet his feet with her tears. Then she wiped them with her hair, kissed them and poured perfume on them.

When the Pharisee who had invited him saw this, he said to himself, "If this man were a prophet, he would know who is touching him and what kind of woman she is—that she is a sinner."

Jesus answered him, "Simon, I have something to tell you."

"Tell me, teacher," he said.

"Two people owed money to a certain moneylender. One owed him five hundred denarii, and the other fifty. Neither of them had the money to pay him back, so he forgave the debts of both. Now which of them will love him more?"

Simon replied, "I suppose the one who had the bigger debt forgiven."

"You have judged correctly," Jesus said.

Then he turned toward the woman and said to Simon, "Do you see this woman? I came into your house. You did not give me any water for my feet, but she wet my feet with her tears and wiped them with her hair. You did not give me a kiss, but this woman, from the time I entered, has not stopped kissing my feet. You did not put oil on my head, but she has poured perfume on my feet. Therefore, I tell you, her many sins have been forgiven—as her great love has shown. But whoever has been forgiven little loves little."

Then Jesus said to her, "Your sins are forgiven."

The other guests began to say among themselves, "Who is this who even forgives sins?"

Jesus said to the woman, "Your faith has saved you; go in peace."

GOD, *help me dig deep into my pockets and heart, giving back all that You have blessed me with. Thank You for pouring out Your love on me, saving me through faith, and offering forgiveness and peace. Amen.*

REFLECT

What can we learn about generosity from this story?

What is one way you can give with soul-deep, love-driven generosity?

Empowered to Do Good

So let's not get tired of doing what is good. At just the right time we will reap a harvest of blessing if we don't give up. Therefore, whenever we have the opportunity, we should do good to everyone—especially to those in the family of faith.

Galatians 6:9–10 NLT

My oldest daughter heard a news report about refugees and asked me about it. I shared with her what I knew, then we looked up more information. We talked about how hard it must be to leave your home and travel to an unfamiliar place, and I reminded her that God commands us to help others. That's when my younger daughter—who happened to be in the room and apparently was all ears—chimed in.

"Mommy! We need to help them! What can we do? I want to help!"

Immediately, my eyes filled with tears, and my heart grew about three sizes. I was so proud of my little girl and moved by her generous heart. But it wasn't long before I also felt myself sighing deeply. How could we help? I didn't know! What I did know was that figuring out how to answer her was going to take time.

I hugged my daughter and told her how happy I was that she wanted to help. I promised to find out how our family could help "the people who left their countries," as she called them.

My experience in working for nonprofit organizations and ministries had taught me that not all help is actually helpful. I'd learned that sometimes helping hurts, and I didn't want to be part of that. I also didn't want to simply throw money at a problem (though as a former fundraiser, I know how crucial financial contributions are). I wanted to find a tangible way for my family to help someone in need, something we could do that would truly make a difference in the life of another. But it turned out that was easier said than done!

I googled and made phone calls and sent emails and asked friends on Facebook. *How can we help?* And every day when she got off the school bus, my little girl asked if I'd found an answer yet. I told her I was waiting for someone to email me back and that I would do another internet search. I told her I was trying.

And I was. I wanted to help too! But I also had a full calendar and a long to-do list, and I was starting to feel a little less warm and fuzzy every time my daughter asked me again how we could help. So I began shrugging off her (and my) desire to do good. Coming up with a plan to help got pushed to the edge of my proverbial plate, and for days at a time I completely forgot about it. Then my daughter brought it up again.

How can we help? Did that lady email you back? What can we do?

Instead of rolling my eyes and sighing in frustration (which I may have been tempted to do), I closed my eyes as I took a deep breath in and breathed out God's name. In that moment I was asking for patience and motivation and guidance. I was asking Him to give me the desire to do good for my daughter and, with her, to do good for others.

Finally, I was spurred back into action. Giving up on the organizations I'd emailed to offer help (who, strangely enough, never did respond), I widened my search and asked another group of friends for ideas. Before I knew it, I had a long list of ways we could help others in our community—plenty of ideas to keep us busy doing good all year long!

Doing good isn't always easy or convenient. We can't always figure out a simple answer to the world's complicated problems. And sometimes feeling too busy or too tired saps our energy for adding one more thing to our list. But God doesn't ask us to do anything He won't make possible. So when doing good feels impossible, it's time to ask God to give us the desire to help, the wisdom to choose how best to help, and the time and energy to make it happen. We ask Him to work in our hearts so we don't get tired of doing good.

Out of obedience and an overflow of God's goodness to us, we press on to goodness. He loves us, so we love others. He helps us, so we help others.

LORD, *thank You for inviting me into the good works You have prepared for me to do. Please give me the desire to do good and the follow-through to keep at it. Use me to show others how much You love them, and may they see You through me. Amen.*

REFLECT

What makes doing good feel impossible to you?

What is one way you can do good today?

Empowered to Be Forgiven

For his unfailing love toward those who fear him
    is as great as the height of the heavens above the
      earth.
He has removed our sins as far from us
    as the east is from the west.
The Lᴏʀᴅ is like a father to his children,
    tender and compassionate to those who fear him.

Psalm 103:11–13 NLT

The day I realized my children could empty the dishwasher was a game changer for me. This almost-daily chore was the bane of my existence, and, much like a child myself, I always put it off in favor of doing anything else. But now my girls could be responsible for putting away our clean dishes while I made dinner or finished up a work project, and it felt like a domestic miracle.

Of course, handing off this chore to my kids meant that I'd occasionally find dishes in the wrong spot—or go for a day or two without being able to find a dish I needed at all! And then there was the inevitable accident, when my youngest dropped a bowl on the kitchen floor. In a split second the ice cream bowl I had painted for my husband at a long-ago paint-your-own-pottery night shattered beyond repair.

Startled at the noise, both our heads snapped up as we stared at each other. Her eyes bounced between my face and the ceramic pieces at her feet as she visibly began to panic. "Mommy! I'm so sorry! I'm sorry, Mommy! It slipped! I'm sorry! Ohhh, I'm sorry!"

"It's okay," I assured her. "What happened? Did something break? Are you okay?"

She told me that she'd dropped a bowl and that it was broken. I instructed her to stand still so she wouldn't step on anything sharp. I told her that it was okay, that accidents happen. Then I walked into the kitchen to clean up the mess and realized which bowl had broken. When I saw that it was my one bowl that's truly irreplaceable, I couldn't hide my disappointment—which my daughter mistook as a sign that she was in trouble.

"I'm sorry . . ." The rush of apologies began once more, as she tripped over her own tongue, trying to make sure I knew how very sorry she felt. She told me again that it had slipped out of her hand, working so hard to convince me that she hadn't broken the bowl on purpose, that she wasn't being neglectful or irresponsible. And I told her again that it was okay, working hard to convince her that I wasn't angry and that I knew these things just happen sometimes.

Round and round we went, her apologizing and me telling her it was okay, as I picked up shards of my pretty bowl and wrapped them up for the trash. For days she apologized and I forgave, nearly to the point of being annoying! As she finally accepted that she was forgiven (or simply forgot the incident), I realized that how she acted is how I often act when I'm the one who needs to apologize.

I do it to my friends and family when I've wronged them, whether it was intentional or as accidental as a little girl dropping a bowl on the kitchen floor. Over and over, I bring up my transgressions and express my deep remorse in an effort to assure them I recognize how badly I messed up.

I do this with the Lord too. As soon as I realize I've sinned against Him, I turn my eyes to His face—shocked, panicked, afraid of the consequences to come. I begin my apologies without taking more than a second or two to reflect on anything other than my regret (and my desire to avoid getting in trouble).

When I'm calm and reasonable, I know my heavenly Father reacts just like I did with my daughter and the broken bowl—compassionate, concerned for my well-being, and merciful. But in the moment I recognize my sin, I'm flooded with regret and fear and immediately begin working to earn His forgiveness.

But forgiveness doesn't work that way. The Lord offers us mercy and pardons our sins not based on the vehemence of our apologies but because of the sacrifice Jesus made when He died for our sins. On the cross He said, "It is finished," not, "Tell me again how sorry you are."

Christ died for us. God forgives us. It is finished.

If you find yourself apologizing over and over, attempting to prove to God or to others just how remorseful you are, may I gently suggest you stop? Our heavenly Father has promised to remove our sin as far as the east is from the west. Believe in Him. Believe in His promise. And accept His forgiveness. Let it stay finished so you can live forgiven.

HEAVENLY FATHER, *thank You for Your mercy. Thank You that I don't have to beg for it but that You give it to me abundantly because of Christ. Forgive me for where I've gone wrong, and please help me trust Your forgiveness and rest in Your compassion toward me. In Jesus's name, amen.*

REFLECT

How do you react when forgiveness is offered?

What sin or situation do you need to let go of and accept forgiveness for today?

The Power of Advocating for Yourself

Numbers 27:1–11

The daughters of Zelophehad approached; Zelophehad was the son of Hepher, son of Gilead, son of Machir, son of Manasseh from the clans of Manasseh, the son of Joseph. These were the names of his daughters: Mahlah, Noah, Hoglah, Milcah, and Tirzah. They stood before Moses, the priest Eleazar, the leaders, and the entire community at the entrance to the tent of meeting and said, "Our father died in the wilderness, but he was not among Korah's followers, who gathered together against the LORD. Instead, he died because of his own sin, and he had no sons. Why should the name of our father be taken away from his clan? Since he had no son, give us property among our father's brothers."

Moses brought their case before the LORD, and the LORD answered him, "What Zelophehad's daughters say is correct. You are to give them hereditary property among their father's brothers and transfer their father's inheritance to them. Tell the Israelites: When a man dies without having a son, transfer his inheritance to his daughter. If he has no daughter, give his inheritance to his brothers. If he has no brothers, give his inheritance to his father's brothers. If his father has no brothers, give his inheritance to the nearest relative of his clan, and he will take possession of it. This is to be a statutory ordinance for the Israelites as the LORD commanded Moses." (CSB)

GOD, *thank You for power to advocate for myself and for others because You first did that for us. Give me the courage to speak up and show up when things are not right or as they should be. Amen.*

REFLECT

What can we learn from this story about the power of advocating for yourself and others?

What is one way you can advocate for yourself or for the people in your life?

Empowered to Be Valued

Our father died in the wilderness. He was not among Korah's followers, who banded together against the LORD, but he died for his own sin and left no sons. Why should our father's name disappear from his clan because he had no son? Give us property among our father's relatives.

Numbers 27:3–4

"It's hard to be seen, let alone respected, as a woman in the workplace—especially as an Asian American woman. Unless I'm wearing a blazer and high heels, the assumption is that I should be the one getting coffee for the group instead of the one leading the meeting."

The rest of us at the table—women of various ethnic backgrounds and across the career spectrum—nod our heads in agreement and lament that this has too often been our experience as well. Unless we appear taller, older, more domineering, or even more masculine, we're not taken seriously or seen as professional.

Another woman shares how she's held back tears in ministry meetings because she knew her opinion would be discounted. She would've been deemed "too emotional," and therefore her empathy and heart for justice would've been overlooked. I can see the anguish and anger in her face when she talks about how powerless and diminished she felt in those situations and how she longed to be valued without repressing her emotions.

I'm stunned by the commonality of our pain. I had thought I was the only one who was seen as "the cute Asian girl" instead of the professional grown woman that I am, and I'm relieved that I'm not alone in feeling overlooked and undervalued.

At five foot one, with a round face, eager smile, and chipper attitude, I feel as though I'm playing dress-up when I take the stage at a conference or sit in leadership meetings where I'm the only woman in the room. I've learned along the way that heels and a blazer *do* make a difference in the way I'm treated and that tears indicate weakness, not strength.

Furthermore, and sadly, I've seen women in Christian spaces who are looked down on for the way they dress if they're highlighting their best physical features or who are laughed at for their intelligence or their courage to fight against misogyny.

I despise that I've needed to and chosen to suppress who I am to some extent in order to fit into the likeness of what others—and especially men—have said about who and how I should be.

My womanhood is not a liability to myself or to anyone else. It is a gift.

I hear this message most clearly from those outside of faith circles, but in the quietest parts of my soul, I know it's true in God's eyes too. Though the stories of the Bible are set within patriarchal cultures, there are glimpses of God's heart for women throughout the arc of Scripture. The daughters of Zelophehad are given their father's inheritance in the promised land right alongside his other male relatives (Num. 27:1–11). Jesus is born of Mary (Luke 1:26–38), and Tamar, Rahab, Ruth, and Bathsheba are all included in His genealogy. Mary Magdalene is the first messenger to bring news of the resurrection (John 20:11–18).

I see myself particularly in the story of Zelophehad's five daughters. Mahlah, Noah, Hoglah, Milkah, and Tirzah have the audacity and the strength of sisterhood to confront Moses, Eleazar the priest, and all the leaders of Israel to demand that they be recognized as legitimate heirs of their father's land. They challenge the cultural expectations, history, and laws of their people, which do not favor women. Moses brings their case before the Lord, and God responds, "What Zelophehad's daughters are saying is right. You must certainly give them property as an inheritance among their father's relatives and give their father's inheritance to them" (Num. 27:7).

Mahlah, Noah, Hoglah, Milkah, and Tirzah knew their value, and they made it known to everyone else. They set a precedent for women to be audacious and valued, and in God's approval of their request, I see His approval of my worth as well.

FATHER, *You see me fully. When You breathed life into me, You breathed pricelessness into me. When it seems that my womanhood is a liability for others, help me to remember that You made me a woman on purpose and that You value me as such. Make me audacious and bold like the daughters of Zelophehad, like Jesus Himself. Amen.*

REFLECT

How have you felt devalued and overlooked by society, in your family, or at work?

How does knowing your God-given value change the way you move in this world?

Empowered to Be Free

So Christ has truly set us free. Now make sure that you stay free, and don't get tied up again in slavery to the law. . . . For you have been called to live in freedom, my brothers and sisters. But don't use your freedom to satisfy your sinful nature. Instead, use your freedom to serve one another in love. For the whole law can be summed up in this one command: "Love your neighbor as yourself."

Galatians 5:1, 13–14 NLT

As we sat in the drive-through, my youngest daughter and I discussed what we would order. A last-minute change in plans meant the two of us were on a dinner date, and we wanted to make the most of it. We'd settled on a burger place with outdoor seating so we'd have a good view of the sunset—my daughter's request. But we planned to buy dessert at the new ice cream shop down the road later. So as we debated which sides to order with our sandwiches, I suggested we go with regular fries, not cheese fries, to balance out the sweet treat we were looking forward to.

"It's your money, Mommy," my daughter said. "You can do whatever you want."

I chuckled to myself because she was right. Technically, I could do whatever I wanted with my money and my meal. And how many times had I done just that? How many times had I ordered the cheese fries *and* the ice cream, both literally and figuratively? That is the right and delight of being a grown-up, after all.

But what my six-year-old didn't know yet—and what I still struggle to remember at times—is that the freedom to make my own choices also comes with the burden of consequences. Like Spider-Man, we all have to learn that with great power comes great responsibility. As Paul reminds the Corinthians, even though everything is permissible, not everything is beneficial (1 Cor. 6:12; 10:23).

While Jesus promises us freedom—in fact, He gave His very life so we could be free—I don't think He intends for us to use it to order all the junk food we want in one night. The freedom He offers us is not what children (or adults) imagine when they shout, "You're not the boss of me!" It's not the freedom we're seeking when we mutter, "You can't tell me what to do," and then willfully walk away from wisdom or obedience. Because though we might convince ourselves that we're our own boss and we can make our own decisions, when that course of action leads us into selfishness, recklessness, or any other brand of disobedience, we've simply enslaved ourselves to sin and whatever consequences come with it.

Jesus said that He came so we could live life to the full (John 10:10), and Paul's words here in Galatians make it clear that a full life, a *free* life, is one where we follow Jesus in order to be set free from sin. While it's easy to swing too far toward one extreme or the other—to legalism (slavery to the law) or to hedonism (slavery to ourselves)—Jesus offers us something else. He has rescued us from the bondage of sin not so we can serve ourselves but so we can serve others.

My daughter was technically correct: I can do whatever I want with my money. I can spend it on cheese fries or ice cream or both. I can buy every new book and graphic tee and all the seasonal decor that catches my eye. I can do whatever I want! And I don't think God is opposed to books or shirts or fall wreaths. But Scripture makes it clear that my freedom—like all the gifts God gives us—is not for me alone. He has set me free so I am better able to love others.

So when I'm deciding how to use my money or time or energy, I can do what I want. But what I want is to be truly free—from temptation, from distraction, from being controlled by my own wishes and whims. And with God, this is possible for each of us. He will give us the desire to use all our gifts and blessings and will place before us opportunities to serve others in love. Only then, when we're released not just from rules or restrictions but also from the trappings of temptation, will we be free.

JESUS, *thank You for living, dying, and rising so I can be free. I want to be truly free—from legalism and hedonism—and use my freedom to serve others. Thank You that You desire an abundant life for me. Help me live in the freedom You've given me in Christ. Amen.*

REFLECT

What is keeping you from living a life of freedom?

What would it look like to accept the freedom Jesus is offering you today?

The Power of Being Seen by Jesus

Mark 5:24–34

So Jesus went with him, and a large crowd was following and pressing against him.

Now a woman suffering from bleeding for twelve years had endured much under many doctors. She had spent everything she had and was not helped at all. On the contrary, she became worse. Having heard about Jesus, she came up behind him in the crowd and touched his clothing. For she said, "If I just touch his clothes, I'll be made well." Instantly her flow of blood ceased, and she sensed in her body that she was healed of her affliction.

Immediately Jesus realized that power had gone out from him. He turned around in the crowd and said, "Who touched my clothes?"

His disciples said to him, "You see the crowd pressing against you, and yet you say, 'Who touched me?'"

But he was looking around to see who had done this. The woman, with fear and trembling, knowing what had happened to her, came and fell down before him, and told him the whole truth. "Daughter," he said to her, "your faith has saved you. Go in peace and be healed from your affliction." (CSB)

LORD, *thank You for seeing me in the fullness of myself and for desiring wholeness in my body, mind, and soul. Amen.*

REFLECT

When have you felt seen by Jesus?

What do you need to bring before Him for healing?

Empowered to Be Kind

Your kindness will reward you, but your cruelty will destroy you.

Proverbs 11:17 NLT

I remember so clearly the day my friend Jane said she needed to talk to me. I walked back to her office and sat down, unaware of the blow that was coming but nervous all the same. She told me that I'd hurt her deeply with an offhand remark someone had overheard and reported to her, and she didn't understand why I'd say such a thing.

Staring at her in shock, my eyes filled with tears and all I could think was, *But I prayed for you!* I couldn't consider how my actions had hurt my friend or how my misconstrued words had the opposite effect of what I intended. All I could think about was how, just a few weeks earlier, I'd prayed around the clock for Jane's family during a crisis. I'd supported her and loved her and been there for her, and now she doubted me. She took the word of another that I had said something to hurt her. My heart was crushed, and my defenses were sky-high. We sat in that room, both of us feeling betrayed and let down by the other.

Though I didn't feel sorry in the moment, I apologized to my friend. And I eventually did understand how the words I'd intended to be kind and encouraging to another friend had, in fact, been hurtful to Jane. Genuinely remorseful, I then apologized to her again.

I realized something after that situation though. This wasn't the first time I'd felt doubly offended by someone I'd prayed for. Not only had they wronged me (at least in my mind), but they did it despite how fervently I'd prayed for them. I realized that I was treating prayer—an intimate act of kindness that, to me, carried enormous relational weight—as a guarantee that the person I prayed for would owe me a similar kindness. Rather than seeing prayer as an unconditional gift on behalf of someone I care about, I saw the act of praying for my friends—or helping them move or throwing them a baby shower or helping them write a résumé or, if I'm honest, any sizable gesture of kindness—as an investment or as friendship insurance.

Somewhere along the way, I began to believe that kindness deserved to be repaid, that kindness was a deposit into a relationship and I'd eventually see dividends returned for my efforts. If you had asked me, I'm certain I would have said that kindness was its own reward, that helping others was how I showed them my love and God's love. But part of me still expected to get what I'd "earned" with all my good deeds and kindness.

Unfortunately, that experience permanently changed my friendship with Jane. But God also used it to begin changing my heart. He showed me that while I was often kind, my motives weren't pure. And He reminded me that I shouldn't expect earthly rewards anyway. During the Sermon on the Mount, Jesus flipped many of His listeners' assumptions upside-down—including how they should treat their enemies. He said, "But love your enemies, do good to them, and lend to them without expecting to get anything back. Then your reward will be great, and you will be children of the Most High, because he is kind to the ungrateful and wicked" (Luke 6:35).

Jesus said our reward for showing kindness—to enemies, yes, but also to friends—would be great. But He never promised that reward in this life. Now, when I read His words and Proverbs 11:17, which promises a reward for kindness, I understand that the reward we receive is a heavenly one. It's the satisfying knowledge that we are acting like our heavenly Father did when He showed us His love by sending His only Son, knowing we could never repay that gift.

Love without strings and kindness without expectations aren't easy. They are impossible, really, unless we ask God to give us His heart for others. Only then will we be able to truly love one another, giving freely and offering kindness as a genuine expression of God's love. And our eternal reward for that will be more than we can imagine.

GOD, *I'm so grateful for Your unconditional kindness. Please forgive me for treating kindness as a transaction, and please give me the strength and love to be kind to others without expecting anything in return. Amen.*

REFLECT

What would it look like for you to show kindness without expecting to be repaid?

How would that feel different from how you've operated in the past?

Empowered to Be Joyful

You reveal the path of life to me;
in your presence is abundant joy;
at your right hand are eternal pleasures.

Psalm 16:11 CSB

Did you know the phrase "dumpster fire" is in the dictionary? In 2018, Merriam-Webster decided this colorful description of disaster was used often enough by enough people that it deserved its own entry.

I suppose I'm not surprised. How many times have I used that phrase to describe a situation or a season? A lot. I've said it a lot.

But lately I've been trying to avoid the saying, which one reporter calls a "gleefully catastrophic phrase."[1] While it remains true—sometimes devastatingly so—that this world offers us constant chaos and catastrophe, that isn't the only truth I know and believe. And it isn't the reality I want to focus on or have a false sense of delight in.

Don't get me wrong. I'm not saying we should deny reality or pretend like everything is fine when it's not. We shouldn't filter our words and our photos so heavily that nobody ever sees our true feelings. And I am certainly not saying it's wrong to grieve or struggle when life is hard. But while it's healthy to feel our feelings and to share openly

1. Renee Klahr, "A Phrase for Our Time: Merriam-Webster Adds 'Dumpster Fire' to Dictionary," MPR News, March 6, 2018, https://www.mprnews.org/story/2018/03/05/npr-a-phrase-for-our-time-merriam-webster-adds-dumpster-fire-to-dictionary.

with trusted friends and family, let's not dive into despair and throw our hope into the dumpster!

When we throw up our hands and declare a situation, a season, an entire calendar year to be a complete loss (i.e., a dumpster fire), we're choosing to abandon hope and walk away from the joy God is placing before us. Instead, we're attempting to find joy in the fleeting—and false—feeling of relief that comes from cursing a hard circumstance and avoiding both the real pain we're experiencing and any gift or beauty that God offers us in the midst of that pain.

My oldest daughter just turned thirteen, and already I'm tired of people telling me how terrible the teen years are. First of all, I'm not so old that I've forgotten the challenges of being a teenager (and the many fights I got into with my mom). Second, and more importantly, I don't like being told that I should expect parenting to be miserable for the next several years.

Thankfully, a few of my friends have children a bit older than mine and have chosen to find joy in parenting their teenagers. When they share about late-night conversations, shared laughs over old movies or autocorrect disasters, or the way having another driver in the house frees up their time (if not their worries), I feel so grateful to see that it's not all bad. I'm encouraged to look for the ways God gives us joy in even the most annoying, awkward, or awful seasons.

At the time I'm writing this, our world resembles a dumpster fire in so many ways. It's hard out there, and to be honest, it's hard in here. Globally and personally, it's been a difficult season—and I'm not sure when it will get better. If ever I've been tempted to throw in the towel and feel confident that joy is nowhere to be found, this is it. But rather than leaning into the cynicism that says nothing good can come from any of this, instead of abandoning my deep belief that we can choose the joy of the Lord in even the darkest times, I'm determined to choose joy.

Are you looking at a world or a season or even a life that you desperately want to declare a waste, a loss, a real dumpster fire? What would it feel like to pause, take a deep breath, and open your heart just enough to be filled with the joy of God's love and His presence in your life? Is it possible to do this?

If you're struggling to find anything good at all, ask God to help. Ask Him to reveal the path of life to you, to open your eyes to the beauty in the middle of the pain, to show you one reason to feel joy. Perhaps it's simply His presence that brings you comfort and then delight. Perhaps He will show you the work He's doing even while chaos seems to reign. Perhaps He will redirect your thoughts to focus on the good gifts He gives us rather than the pain of this world.

Finding joy when everything is falling apart (or burning) feels impossible, but nothing is impossible for our God. Ask Him to be with you and to bring you joy, and He will do it.

LORD, *thank You for never abandoning me or this world when we seem like a lost cause. Please give me the strength to feel my feelings but to also keep going, to search for beauty, and to find joy—no matter my circumstances. Give me eyes to see You wherever I look today. Amen.*

REFLECT

When have you struggled to find something good?

What is one thing—huge or small or anywhere in between—that brought you joy this week?

The Power of Including Women

Luke 8:1–3

After this, Jesus traveled about from one town and village to another, proclaiming the good news of the kingdom of God. The Twelve were with him, and also some women who had been cured of evil spirits and diseases: Mary (called Magdalene) from whom seven demons had come out; Joanna the wife of Chuza, the manager of Herod's household; Susanna; and many others. These women were helping to support them out of their own means.

> **LORD**, *thank You for valuing women, for seeing the power in our presence, friendship, and partnership. Help me not to shrink back when You invite me to partner with You in the work that You're doing. Amen.*

REFLECT

What can we learn about God's perspective of women from this Scripture passage?

How can you partner with God in the work He is doing to redeem the world?

Empowered to Face Despair

Why, my soul, are you downcast?
    Why so disturbed within me?
Put your hope in God,
    for I will yet praise him,
    my Savior and my God.
My soul is downcast within me;
    therefore I will remember you
from the land of the Jordan,
    the heights of Hermon—from Mount Mizar.

Psalm 42:5–6

The screaming and crying are high-pitched and unbearable. I don't understand why my baby has regressed. Why isn't she going to sleep as easily as before? Is it teething? A growth spurt? A nightmare? Instead of the twelve hours of quiet and rest I used to get, now every night I sit in the hallway outside her closed door, listening to her wail and waiting for her to go back to sleep. My stubbornness and rigidity to stick to the schedule keeps me from going in, but my new-mother heart keeps me seated, unbudging.

I clench my teeth and pound my fists on my thighs. I cover my ears and rock back and forth. I pull my hair. I want it to end. I want to be able to sleep without interruption or worry that she'll wake up her daddy, who works the swing shift and is barely getting sleep as it is.

I want her to get the rest she needs because she's just a baby. I throw my whys and hows at God, demanding answers and getting silence.

Eventually, the crying mercifully ends, and I leave my post in the hallway. I trudge downstairs, my legs heavy. My eyelids too. But my heart is still racing, and my ears ring even in the quiet. I feel the threads of my sanity unraveling, and I feel imprisoned by despair, by the lack of reprieve, by this part of mothering.

My husband is working. I'm alone. And the thoughts begin:

I just want to sleep—is that too much to ask?

I wish I could disappear into a void where no one needs me.

I want to disappear.

I need to disappear.

I sink deeper and start to wonder how I can do this in the most considerate way, with the least amount of cleanup for my husband when he finds me. Falling asleep in the car with the engine running in the garage sounds enticing, doable.

But as I realize how far I've come in my suicidal ideation, I scare myself. My heart beats in my ears as I pick up the phone and send out a mass text in the middle of the night to friends near and far:

Please pray for me. I'm having suicidal thoughts.

Typing out the words brings a flood of shame. The critic is loud in my head, telling me I should be embarrassed, that I hadn't gone far enough to warrant a call for help. But with each text that comes through from friends saying they're praying for me, light and fresh air enter the darkness—I'm not alone.

When we're deep in depression, overwhelmed with life, or stuck in impossible situations, hope feels like wishful thinking. In Psalm 42:5–6, the psalmist urges his soul to hope in God. He's not chiding himself to *feel* hope right there in the depths of his despair. He's saying, "One day—someday—I will praise God again, so soul, hope in Him." He's looking to a future deliverance, and he's certain that God will see to it.

In the meantime, he remembers God from his place of despair. We have the whole of history to look back on and see how God has been faithful. Recounting the truths He's spoken to us and the ways His presence carried us makes hope substantial. And God Himself understands darkness and death. Christ experienced it in His body on the cross, and so our hope in Him is not like a thin silver lining. Instead, it's like a thick rope thrown down to lift us out of the pit—to take another step and live another day.

GOD, *thank You for understanding despair and for not being afraid of death. You enter into the darkness and sit with me instead of scolding me and forcing me toward the light. You are gentle in Your care, and You provide a way out—even if it's not in my timing or in a way I can fathom. Help me to have the long view of "someday" to make me resilient when I can't see beyond my pain. Amen.*

REFLECT

If you or someone you love struggles with depression and suicidal ideation, how could Psalm 42:5–6 give hope to keep going?

Looking back on your life or over the whole of history, how have you seen God's presence and faithfulness?

If you or someone you love struggles with depression and suicidal thoughts, please reach out to a trusted person and seek professional help. The National Suicide Prevention Lifeline is available 24 hours a day at 1–800–273–8255.

Empowered to Be Surrendered

"For I know the plans I have for you," says the LORD. "They are plans for good and not for disaster, to give you a future and a hope. In those days when you pray, I will listen. If you look for me whole-heartedly, you will find me. I will be found by you," says the LORD.

Jeremiah 29:11–14 NLT

When I was in high school, I taped a poster of the New York City sky-line on the wall directly across from my bed. It caught my eye every day as I thought, "Someday . . ."

I dreamed of traveling to the Big Apple, but that poster represented more than my hopes for a fun vacation. For as long as I could remember, my goal in life was to escape my small hometown—the place I'd grown up sheltered and safe, the place I'd felt stifled and held back. Surely living in a big city would allow me to become the person I was meant to be!

By the time I graduated from college, my dreams had changed a bit and my priorities had shifted. Still, I strained against the confines of the life I was beginning to build, resenting the limits on what I really wanted to do, where I really wanted to go, who I really wanted to be. So I made plans and set goals. I researched options and fueled my desire to do more, go more, be more. And I prayed. I prayed that God would help me fulfill the potential He'd given me by blessing the plans I was making. I asked Him to open doors and clear paths. I begged Him to take me anywhere other than where I was—another small town so far in every way from the glittery skylines I'd imagined for myself.

He said no.

Over and over, my plans went unfulfilled. My goals remained unmet. And I grew even more desperate to force what I believed was my destiny, my great calling, to become reality. I didn't want to live where I lived or work where I worked; I wished for a new life, a different path. But that wasn't actually what God had planned for me.

It took time—so much time!—but eventually I realized that, while God could have certainly used me to do great things for His kingdom had I traveled far away from where I started, He could also use me right here. Like the Israelites in the book of Jeremiah, I began to hear God's whisper to stay where I'd been planted instead of striving to escape (Jer. 29:4–7). I began to understand that He can use me where I am, far from the glittering lights and childhood dreams.

When God says He has good plans for us, we often think those plans are the same ones we've made for ourselves. We pray and wait for God to bless our goals, to turn our dreams into reality. But the reality is that He has a good plan for us, the best plan for us—and it's almost always something we never could have dreamed up on our own. Surrendering to that truth has been one of the hardest lessons I've learned. If I'm painfully honest, it's one I'm still learning today.

I don't really love the town where I live. The work I do is adjacent to my dream job but not quite what I've had in mind and heart all these years. Nothing is quite like I imagined it would be, but it remains clear that this is where God has placed me—on purpose and for a purpose.

So I turn away from the temptation of resentment and striving, and I ask God to show me His good plan for me. I ask Him to help me surrender to His plans, His purpose, His place for me in this world. I ask God to help me love the people in my community and serve people right where I am, right where they are. I ask Him to protect me from bitterness or envy, to remove my desire to be anywhere other than where He wants me to be.

Then I do it all over again the next day. Because surrendering to God's will isn't a one-and-done act; it's a day-by-day, minute-by-minute sacrifice of self in obedience to the One who created me. It's asking Him as many times as it takes to change my heart and keep my eyes on Him and on His plans instead of my own.

GOD, *thank You for having a good plan for me. Sometimes it's hard to remember that Your plans are so much better than what I can dream up. Please help me let go of my desires, and make Your will the desire of my heart today. Amen.*

REFLECT

What is God asking you to let go of today?

What would it look like to turn away from your own plans and desires and surrender to His?

The Power of Witnessing Glory

John 20:1–18

Early on the first day of the week, while it was still dark, Mary Magdalene went to the tomb and saw that the stone had been removed from the entrance. So she came running to Simon Peter and the other disciple, the one Jesus loved, and said, "They have taken the Lord out of the tomb, and we don't know where they have put him!"

So Peter and the other disciple started for the tomb. Both were running, but the other disciple outran Peter and reached the tomb first. He bent over and looked in at the strips of linen lying there but did not go in. Then Simon Peter came along behind him and went straight into the tomb. He saw the strips of linen lying there, as well as the cloth that had been wrapped around Jesus' head. The cloth was still lying in its place, separate from the linen. Finally the other disciple, who had reached the tomb first, also went inside. He saw and believed. (They still did not understand from Scripture that Jesus had to rise from the dead.) Then the disciples went back to where they were staying.

Now Mary stood outside the tomb crying. As she wept, she bent over to look into the tomb and saw two angels in white, seated where Jesus' body had been, one at the head and the other at the foot.

They asked her, "Woman, why are you crying?"

"They have taken my Lord away," she said, "and I don't know where they have put him." At this, she turned around and saw Jesus standing there, but she did not realize that it was Jesus.

He asked her, "Woman, why are you crying? Who is it you are looking for?"

Thinking he was the gardener, she said, "Sir, if you have carried him away, tell me where you have put him, and I will get him."

Jesus said to her, "Mary."

She turned toward him and cried out in Aramaic, "Rabboni!" (which means "Teacher").

Jesus said, "Do not hold on to me, for I have not yet ascended to the Father. Go instead to my brothers and tell them, 'I am ascending to my Father and your Father, to my God and your God.'"

Mary Magdalene went to the disciples with the news: "I have seen the Lord!" And she told them that he had said these things to her.

LORD, *thank You for choosing Mary Magdalene to be the first witness of the resurrection. It tells me so much about the way You see, value, and elevate women. You entrust us and empower us, and I'm ready to do what You're calling me to do too. Amen.*

REFLECT

Why is it so important that God chose Mary Magdalene to be the first person to see the resurrected Jesus?

How does Mary Magdalene being the first to share the good news of the resurrection inspire you to share the gospel too?

Empowered to Be Generous

Jesus sat down opposite the place where the offerings were put and watched the crowd putting their money into the temple treasury. Many rich people threw in large amounts. But a poor widow came and put in two very small copper coins, worth only a few cents. Calling his disciples to him, Jesus said, "Truly I tell you, this poor widow has put more into the treasury than all the others. They all gave out of their wealth; but she, out of her poverty, put in everything—all she had to live on."

Mark 12:41–44

In college, I had an internship with the youth ministry program at a local church. I worked with the middle school and high school students, and eventually I took over the program when the youth director left. One day I attended a staff meeting that was to be focused on stewardship and giving. Honestly, I thought I would just smile and nod, because I was a fresh-out-of-college, broke young woman who worked with the youth. I didn't think there was any way a conversation about generous giving could pertain to me.

I was sorely mistaken.

The conversation began with how we could continue cultivating a spirit of financial generosity in our congregation. As that discussion wound up, I figured we were done. But then another staff member brought out a blue piece of paper. "Okay, let's update the time and talents sheet!" she chirped.

An identical blue sheet of paper had been given to every member of our church to fill out and indicate their volunteer capacity and interests. People could sign up to staff the nursery or sing in the choir, lead a book club or organize the annual food drive. There were signups for mowing the lawn and cleaning the sanctuary, cooking freezer meals for community members in need, and volunteering to serve dinner each Wednesday night before worship. They could sign up to be on the usher team, welcoming people to worship on Sunday mornings. People could offer their skills and play an instrument in the worship band, run the soundboard, or put together the lyric slides.

I realized the church wasn't asking for people simply to give of their treasures. They were asking people to dig a little deeper and give offerings of themselves.

Time and talents.

Those three words struck me because I had previously thought that being generous could only happen if you were rich and had cash to spare. A whole new world opened up for me!

At that point in my life, I truly didn't have cash to spare. But I had time to give, and so I gave it. I started to see mine as an offering of time, and I began to reach out in other ways to share my talents— singing with the band, leading a new ministry for young moms, and starting a craft night.

More than a decade later, my husband and I were praying about our offering to our church. For a long time, we lived stretching one paycheck into another, staying within our means but just barely. We were able to give what we considered to be the minimum. But after a few years, new jobs, raises, and some financial reorganizing, we recognized that we could comfortably up our annual contribution.

However, we weren't really okay with being comfortable anymore. We realized that God was calling us to give more, and not just of our treasures. He was calling us to dig deeply into our community, our church, our friendships, and to give more of our own selves.

It's one thing to give a large sum and not be affected by the money coming out of the checking account each month. It's another thing to give sacrificially—to truly dig a little deeper and give until we actually feel that stretch. It's then that we may also feel the peace of God because we're giving all the way from our heart.

Maybe it's a monetary gift to a meaningful charity or an organization close to your heart. Maybe it's a sacrifice of time, volunteering on a Saturday morning rather than sleeping in. Maybe it's gulping down nerves and playing a solo for special music during your church service one Sunday.

Whatever the gift is, whether it's time, treasure, or talent, Jesus wants it to come from the heart. It matters to Him that we feel the offering in some way. Like the widow giving everything she had to live on, we too can give until it hurts.

God will meet us in our generosity, and because of His graciousness and generous spirit, we can give from our hearts.

LORD, *help me dig deep in my giving. Thank You for creating so many ways that we can be generous. Thank You that because of Your generous heart I am empowered to give of my time, talent, and treasures. Give me the wisdom to discern which to offer and when. Amen.*

REFLECT

What's one way you can give as the widow did—deeply and from your heart?

How is God calling you to give—your time, your talent, and/or your treasures?

Empowered to Be Who God Made Us to Be

The LORD God said, "It is not good for the man to be alone. I will make a helper suitable for him."

Genesis 2:18

I sat in the sanctuary with a hundred other women, listening to a sermon unlike any I'd heard before. Tears streamed down my face as I learned for the first time who I was created to be as a woman made in the image of God. *How had I missed out on this truth all my life?* I was in my midthirties and had grown up in the church, and somehow the message I heard most about Eve was that she was the one to blame for the downfall of humanity. She had been the one who was tempted, the one who first ate the fruit, the one who enticed Adam to eat with her.

She was weak, lesser than Adam, and the lesson I often heard was that I shouldn't be like her. Even worse, *because* I was a woman, I couldn't help but be like her. I considered it a thorn in my flesh that I was born female instead of male, and in order to compensate for my supposedly inherent weakness, I needed to prove my strength.

Yet here I was listening to a sermon that upended all of that. The message honed in on the phrase "a helper suitable for him" translated from the Hebrew *ezer kenegdo*. Definitions and nuanced meanings of words are often lost in translation when going from one language to another. If we were to look at each word, *kenegdo* means "opposite" or "parallel to" or "equal,"[1] and *ezer* means much more than the limited English translation "helper."

In her book *More Than Enchanting*, Jo Saxton explains that "*ezer* has more to do with what helping looks like, because it doesn't seem to suggest anything about hierarchy. In some instances, *ezer* is a word with military connotations; the *ezer* is also a warrior. In this context, help comes from one who has the power and strength to provide it. *Ezer* is a verb as well as a noun, meaning 'to defend, protect, surround and cherish.' The *ezer* is an amazing mix of strength, power, proactivity, and vulnerability."[2]

Before Adam gives Eve her name, before the fall of humankind in Genesis 3, before Eve is even created by the hand and breath of God, God gives her an identity. She is *ezer kenegdo*, a strong warrior, empowered to help, defend, protect, and cherish as equal to her partner.

I closed my eyes and let the truth baptize me anew. In that half hour, God began healing so many of the faulty narratives I had believed in—not by stitching together what was broken but by giving me a completely new understanding. My feminine heritage wasn't one of weakness but of strength, not one of timidity but of power. From the beginning of time and creation, this was what it meant to be a woman.

I went home that day, awakened and hungry, and started my own search on the word *ezer*. I read articles and wrote down all the Scripture references where *ezer* was used. Twice it's used to refer to Eve, but most of the references thereafter use it to refer to God as our helper, deliverer, defender, and strength (Exod. 18:4; Deut. 33:7, 26, 29; Ps. 20:2; 33:20; 70:5; 89:19; 115:9–11; 121:1–2; 124:8; 146:5; Hos. 13:9).

I was stunned by this revelation. God used the same word for Eve that He used for Himself. Thus, being made in the image of God meant being an *ezer*, and living into the full meaning of *ezer kenegdo* is the way I reflect His image.

1. Jo Saxton, *More Than Enchanting* (Downers Grove, IL: InterVarsity, 2012), 35.
2. Saxton, *More Than Enchanting*, 36.

I scribbled these notes down in my journal, and the tears began afresh. God had begun the healing process, but there was a long road ahead for me to fully embrace this identity. I rested my head on my desk, and a familiar psalm rose in my soul:

> I lift up my eyes to the mountains—
>   where does my help come from?
> My help comes from the LORD,
>   the Maker of heaven and earth. (Ps. 121:1–2)

God is my *Ezer*, and He will help me become who I was made to be.

GOD, *thank You for making me in Your image, and that from the very beginning You created me to be a strong warrior. I am not less-than or weaker because I am a woman, and I praise You for being my helper, my defender, and my Creator. Empower me to reflect Your image more fully in my strength, my vulnerability, my tenderness, and my power. I praise You for I truly am fearfully and wonderfully made (Ps. 139:14). Amen.*

REFLECT

How has a partial interpretation of the word *helper* diminished your understanding of who you were made to be?

How does knowing you're an *ezer* empower you to be more fully yourself?

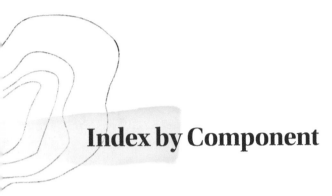

Index by Component

Spiritual

Index by Author

About the Authors

Mary Carver writes and speaks with humor and honesty, encouraging women with truth found in unexpected places. She hosts a podcast about pop culture and faith and is a regular contributor to (in)courage. She is also the author of *Women of Courage, Journey to the Cross*, and the (in)courage Bible study *Courageous Joy*, and the coauthor of *Choose Joy* and *Sacred Tears*. Mary lives for good books, spicy queso, and Hallmark movies, but she lives because of God's grace. She resides in Kansas City with her husband and two daughters, and you can find her online @marycarver and at marycarver.com.

Grace P. Cho is a Korean American writer, poet, and speaker, and the editorial manager at (in)courage. In the middle of her years as a pastor, she felt a pull toward using her words to lead others in a broader context. She believes storytelling can create movements that change the world and desires to elevate the voices of women of color in the publishing industry and in the church. Grace is the coeditor of *Take Heart: 100 Devotions to Seeing God When Life's*

Not Okay and the author of the (in)courage Bible study *Courageous Influence*. Learn more @gracepcho and at gracepcho.com.

Anna E. Rendell writes encouragement to celebrate the ordinary glory found in our everyday. She's the author of *A Moment of Christmas* and *Pumpkin Spice for Your Soul*, the coauthor of *Fake Snow and Real Faith*, editor of *A Mother's Love*, and coeditor of *Take Heart: 100 Devotions to Seeing God When Life's Not Okay*. Anna works as the digital content manager at (in)courage and lives in Minnesota with her husband and their four kids. She loves a good book, a great latte, and walking her dog (not all at once). Find her online @annaerendell and at annarendell.com.

(in)

(in)courage welcomes you

to a place where authentic, brave women connect deeply with God and others. Through the power of shared stories and meaningful resources, (in)courage champions women and celebrates the strength Jesus gives to live out our calling as God's daughters. Together we build community, celebrate diversity, and **become women of courage**.

Join us at **www.incourage.me** and connect with us on social media!

100 Days of Hope and Peace

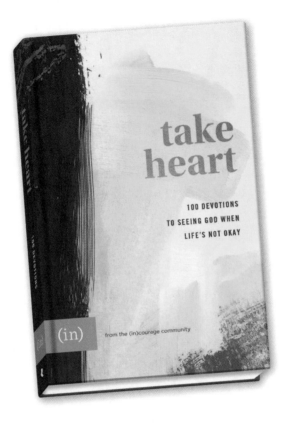

In this 100-day devotional, the (in)courage community reaches into the grief and pain of both crisis and ordinary life. Each day includes a key Scripture, a heartening devotion, and a prayer to remind you that God is near and hope is possible. You won't find tidy bows or trite quick fixes, just arrows pointing you straight to Jesus.

Revell
a division of Baker Publishing Group
www.RevellBooks.com

Available wherever books and ebooks are sold.

Bible Studies to Refresh Your Soul

In these six-week Bible studies, your friends at (in)courage will help you dive deep into real-life issues, the transforming power of God's Word, and what it means to courageously live your faith.

Revell
a division of Baker Publishing Group
www.RevellBooks.com

Available wherever books and ebooks are sold.

New Women's Bible Study Series from the (in)courage Community

This six-week Bible study series from (in)courage pairs Scripture with story, inviting us into a deeper experience of God's Word. Packed with solid observation, interpretation, and application of Scripture, plus daily prayers and memorization, each study strengthens the partnership between us and God.

 **Revell**
a division of Baker Publishing Group
www.RevellBooks.com

Available wherever books and ebooks are sold.